"The Nicene Creed has been a bastion of orthodoxy for 1,700 years, affirming the biblical truth of the full deity of Jesus and the Holy Spirit. This accessible and engaging book brings to life the circumstances surrounding the creation and aftermath of this historic confession. It is a must-read for believers seeking to deepen their understanding of the doctrine of the Trinity and how the church came to define it."

Heinrich Johnsen, president, Christian Art Publishing

"In *The Story of the Trinity*, Bryan M. Litfin masterfully shows that the better you understand the Trinity, the better you will understand the gospel, and the better you understand the gospel, the better you will understand the Trinity. In this wonderfully helpful and readable book, Litfin shows that theology does not develop in a vacuum but in the often messy process of church history. In this book, you will find biblically grounded thinking, enlightening historical theology, and devotional insights that nourish the soul."

Erik Thoennes, PhD, professor of theology, Talbot School of Theology, Biola University; pastor, Grace Evangelical Free Church of La Mirada

"This book is riddled with so many biblical truisms about the character and compassion of our Creator Redeemer, I found myself *amen*ing out loud before finishing the first chapter! And while his doctrinal content is substantive, Dr. Litfin's writing style is refreshingly unstuffy. He generously puts the proverbial cookies of creedal theology on a shelf where everyone can enjoy them and lean further into the unconditional love of our Triune God as a result. In my experience as an oft-bumbling Christ follower, vocational Bible teacher, and doctoral candidate, it's a glorious gift to get to sit at the feet of a brilliant theological scholar who has the tender heart of a pastor. *The Story of the Trinity* is that kind of experience."

Lisa Harper, bestselling author, speaker, and host of the
Back Porch Theology podcast

"Bryan M. Litfin's exhaustive new study of the history of the Nicene Council and its creed, a study I highly recommend, appropriately appears on the 1,700th anniversary of that council. How encouraging to observe such a rigorous study from a well-known evangelical theologian!"

Patrick Henry Reardon, senior editor, *Touchstone:
A Journal of Mere Christianity*

"In my experience, many readers are overwhelmed by theological jargon about the Trinity or the person and work of Jesus Christ. If this describes you, then let Bryan M. Litfin be your guide. *The Story of the Trinity* is a masterclass in distilling biblical, theological, and historical content into an engaging and enjoyable narrative of cosmic proportions. Skeptics and believers alike will profit from Litfin's charm and sagacity. Whether you are a new convert or a seasoned disciple, *The Story of the Trinity* will eloquently and lovingly guide you toward the shores of truth amid the spiritual storms of life."

Coleman M. Ford, PhD, assistant professor of humanities,
Southwestern Baptist Theological Seminary

"Bryan M. Litfin's *The Story of the Trinity* offers a clear, engaging exploration of the Trinity and its central role in salvation. Tracing Old Testament monotheism, the divinity of Jesus, and the Nicene debates, Litfin connects ancient theology to the heart of the Christian gospel. This work invites readers to understand the eternal relationship within God and its implications for human salvation, offering a compelling reflection on God's love as revealed in Jesus Christ."

Karin Spiecker Stetina, PhD, professor of theology, Talbot School of Theology, Biola University

"*The Story of the Trinity* is a marvelous resource, introducing readers to the historical, ecclesial, and political contexts related to the Councils of Nicaea (325) and Constantinople (381). Offering careful and contextual insights regarding the participants and the theological issues, Bryan M. Litfin has given us an excellent introduction to and exposition of the Nicene Creed. I am delighted to recommend this thoughtful, timely, accessible, and carefully presented work."

David S. Dockery, president, International Alliance for Christian Education; president and distinguished professor of theology, Southwestern Baptist Theological Seminary

"Dr. Litfin has written an engaging, learned, and accessible story of the Trinity through the lens of the Nicene Creed and the biblical witness. Readers will discover much that is edifying, insightful, and uplifting to the glory of God! In our day of theological laxity and sometimes waywardness, it is so important that we root our faith in what is substantial and true and have a full grasp in particular of the biblical and historical teaching of the Trinity. Read and enjoy!"

Dr. Josh Moody, senior pastor, College Church in Wheaton; president, God Centered Life Ministries

THE STORY
OF THE TRINITY

THE STORY OF THE TRINITY

CONTROVERSY, CRISIS, AND THE CREATION OF THE NICENE CREED

BRYAN M. LITFIN

BakerBooks

a division of Baker Publishing Group
Grand Rapids, Michigan

Published by Baker Books
a division of Baker Publishing Group
Grand Rapids, Michigan
BakerBooks.com

Printed in the United States of America

Library of Congress Cataloging-in-Publication Data
Names: Litfin, Bryan M., 1970– author
Title: The story of the Trinity : controversy, crisis, and the creation of the Nicene Creed / Bryan M. Litfin.
Description: Grand Rapids, Michigan : Baker Books, a division of Baker Publishing Group, [2025] | Includes bibliographical references.
Identifiers: LCCN 2024051216 | ISBN 9781540904829 paperback | ISBN 9781540905185 casebound | ISBN 9781493451128 ebook
Subjects: LCSH: Trinity—History of doctrines—Early church, ca. 30–600 | Nicene Creed
Classification: LCC BT109 .L58 2025 | DDC 231/.044—dc23/eng/20250416
LC record available at https://lccn.loc.gov/2024051216

Cover design by Chris Kuhatschek

Baker Publishing Group publications use paper produced from sustainable forestry practices and postconsumer waste whenever possible.

25   26   27   28   29   30   31   7   6   5   4   3   2   1

Contents

Foreword

I recently spoke about the Trinity to an adult Sunday school class at a Protestant church, and a friend in the class later filled me in on the chatter my talk elicited. The gist of it was, "Wow, the Trinity is in the Bible!" The surprise those Christians felt that day apparently came from some sort of deep-seated unease they had previously harbored about the Trinity—that the whole business was a philosophical or theological abstraction, foreign to the Scriptures and irrelevant to Christian life. I'm afraid that many sincere Christians today feel this unease.

Such a sense of unease about the Trinity is aggravated in at least two ways. First is the way we talk about the Trinity among ourselves as ordinary believers. Somehow or other, we've imbibed the idea that the Trinity is a math problem, a question about how one can logically put oneness and threeness together without sounding like an idiot. So we latch onto any instances of oneness and threeness we can find down here in this world, and we say, "See, if oneness and threeness come together in X, then they can come together in God too." So we talk about water (gas, liquid, and solid phases at the same time) or eggs (yolk, white, and shell, but one egg) or shamrocks (three branches but one leaf) or even—and I am not making this up—chocolate milkshakes (milk, ice cream, and chocolate, but one drink). We *may* avoid sounding like idiots when we talk like this, but unfortunately we give the impression—to ourselves as well as to outsiders—that such math games have little to do with the gospel and nothing to do with Christian living.

A second way in which Christians' unease about the Trinity gets aggravated is much more serious. There have been many scholars in the past couple of centuries who have insisted that the Trinity is *not* in the Bible, that Jesus was a great man but no more, and that the idea of Christ as God was an invention of fourth-century Christians. Some have even said that the church arbitrarily decided the deity of Christ *by a vote* at the Council of Nicaea in 325. While these modern scholarly opinions tend to circulate in the rarefied air of academic discussion, enough leaks out to the public that many of us Christians are disturbed at some level. We are scared that it might really be true that the church invented a divine Christ several centuries after Jesus's earthly life ended. Deep down, we realize that if that were actually the case, it would blow a hole in our Christian faith so big that it could never be patched up. And we'd be right, *if that were the case.*

If you have such unease or reservations, then this book is for you. In plain-speaking, clear language, Litfin shows that the understanding of the Trinity put forward during the fourth century in the Nicene Creed is not a departure from Scripture but is deeply rooted in God's revelation of himself to mankind—in the New Testament and even in the Old.

This book takes you on a journey that starts at the very beginning of the Bible and continues all the way through both Testaments and beyond, to the end of the fourth century when the Christian church put the finishing touches on what we now call the Nicene Creed. This Creed is the preeminent short statement outside the Bible itself about the Father, Son, and Spirit, as well as about the incarnation and work of the Son for our salvation. It is a profoundly universal statement, since it was accepted at the time by every group of Christians in the world that has subsequently continued to exist. In fact, it is the only statement outside the Bible approved by the entire Christian church. As a result, the Nicene Creed is worthy of our attention, not as a replacement for the Bible or as a challenge to its unique authority, but as an interpretation of the Bible—indeed, as the universal interpretation of the Bible given by the whole Christian church.

The journey on which Litfin takes you is not an easy one; it will stretch you. You'll have to learn some new words in Hebrew, Greek, and even Latin. You'll have to come to grips with the fact that the Bible was not *always* crystal clear about the Trinity, and you'll have to be content with hints of the Trinity in the Old Testament that became clearer in the New. You'll need to accept the fact that not every early Christian reading the Bible got it all right in the first few centuries; Litfin is honest about the mistakes that some early theologians made, as well as about the things they got right. After all, if the Trinity is not easy for *us* to grasp, it wasn't easy for them either! And they were the first ones ever to try to express it without being inspired by the Holy Spirit the way the biblical writers were, so we can imagine that it was even harder for them than for us.

Nevertheless, we *do* see God's Word (the Son) and his Breath (the Holy Spirit) in the Old Testament, if not always clearly. We do see the Son and the Spirit clearly in the New Testament. And slowly but surely, with some false steps along the way, the Christian thinkers of the first few centuries learned from the Scriptures how to write about God, his Son, his Spirit, and the salvation we have. The Nicene Creed was the most significant result of all that thinking and learning.

I invite you to join Litfin on this journey through the Bible and through early Christian thinking about God and about Christian salvation. While it may be tough going at times, I urge you to press on, for it will be worth it. You'll emerge, like that Sunday school class, encouraged that the Trinity is indeed in the Bible and that the Spirit-filled people of the early Christian centuries did indeed learn how to speak of the Trinity clearly and simply. Your mind will be stretched, but your heart will be warmed, and most important, your faith strengthened. Please do turn the page and go to it.

Donald Fairbairn, Robert E. Cooley Professor of Early Christianity at Gordon-Conwell Theological Seminary, professor of historical and systematic theology at Union School of Theology in Wales, and author of *The Story of Creeds and Confessions*, *Life in the Trinity*, and *The Trinity*

Introduction

W hat must I do to be saved?"
        This timeless question was asked long ago by
        a terrified Roman soldier who thought he was
about to die. He had been assigned to guard the prison in the
ancient town of Philippi. Unfortunately for him, an earth-
quake had shaken the building's foundations, cracked open
the doors, and loosened the prisoners' chains. Surely the
inmates had escaped. The penalty for such a failure—even
if it was caused by a natural disaster—was always death.

Amazingly, however, the prisoners hadn't fled. They had
been listening to hymns sung by two Christian evangelists,
Paul and Silas. Just as the jailer was about to plunge a sword
into his breast rather than face the cruel machine of Roman
justice, Paul's voice rang out from the rubble: "Do not harm
yourself, for we are all here" (Acts 16:28).

After calling for lamps, the jailer rushed into the dungeon
to discover that, sure enough, his captives were still inside.
The man fell flat on his face before these two supposed crimi-
nals whose bold witness had spared his life. Such a close
brush with death made the jailer fear for his eternal soul,

prompting his question about where to find salvation. Paul's answer was simple: "Believe in the Lord Jesus, and you will be saved, you and your household" (v. 31).

The Quest for Salvation

Human beings have always sought a remedy for their mortality. Death is the one universal experience that looms over every person. The idea of an afterlife—the ability to go on living after earthly life comes to an end—has entered everyone's mind. Even atheists consider it, though they profess not to care. But most people are religious. They seek an afterlife through some kind of supernatural means. Among the earth's vast population, 2.4 billion people believe that Paul's answer was the right one: Belief in Jesus is the way to be saved.

This book is about that salvation. No, it's not a gospel tract that will lay out the steps you need to climb in order to reach heaven. There will be no call to the altar, no urgent plea to raise your hand or say a prayer, no threatening of imminent fire and brimstone. I'm not going to preach at you. Even so, I repeat: This book is about salvation—and about how Jesus of Nazareth is a central part of it.

I say this to you at the outset, and I say it clearly, because the title of this book identifies its subject as the Nicene Creed and the doctrine of the Trinity. You might be tempted to think this book is essentially about ancient philosophies and obscure dogmas. You might assume the issues we will discuss were concocted by bored people from the olden days who wanted to debate irrelevant trivia. Of course, you will learn about ancient creeds, councils, and church fathers whose names you may never have heard of. And to be honest with you, yes, you will learn about doctrine. But my point is that this book isn't essentially about *theories*. It's about eternal salvation and how to find it.

The Trinity as Gospel

The doctrine of the Trinity—that there is one God who exists eternally as three distinct persons—wasn't developed in a classroom so theologians could have something really weird to quiz their students about. Nor was it formulated for elite philosophers and therefore irrelevant to most people's lives. Just the opposite! The Trinity came to be recognized when regular human beings (not just Christians, but the Jews before them) thought deeply about the nature of God, the problems of man, and the afterlife and how to reach it.

Eventually, those big ideas found expression in a succinct statement from an ancient church meeting called the Council of Nicaea. It happened during the summer of the year 325. The brief theological statement produced by the council (in a slightly later, restated form) is what we today call the Nicene Creed. The attendees didn't assemble at Nicaea to squabble about trifles. Their goal wasn't to win an argument against other skillful debaters. The council fathers realized they were discussing the very nature of the gospel. Nicene Trinitarianism was found to be the best explanation of Christian salvation.

In the Nicene Creed you won't find a specific method to reach God. The ancient Christians understood that a proper explanation of salvation shouldn't begin with the *how* but the *who*. That's why these debates were so intense. They were often treated as if life or death hinged on a single letter (and at one point, it actually did, as you'll learn a bit later). These early Christians were articulating, as best they could, who God is and how Jesus of Nazareth related to him. They knew full well that eternal salvation would depend on how they answered. Does Jesus himself have what it takes to get you all the way to heaven? Or is he just another in a long list of divinely empowered revealers who show the way to

God? Is he a signpost along the road or the actual vehicle that can get you home?

Let me explain further what I mean. Consider two possible views of God and the type of savior each would require. Imagine that God is "up there" in a remote place where humans have to ascend to him by diligent moral effort. He is a distant being and therefore hard to reach, maybe even hard to know. If God is like that, we would expect him to send us an accurate and articulate revealer of himself. But this savior couldn't be God himself, for God is—according to this definition—totally and inevitably remote. That's just his nature, say those who hold this theological view. God doesn't come down here to earth. A descent like that isn't worthy of such an exalted being. So God would have to send a somewhat lesser being—a messenger who isn't God himself—in order to reveal himself to humans.

On the other hand, if the being who is "up there" is the sort of God who involves himself in his creation and sometimes even enters it, then the savior he sends could be equal to God and united with him. This savior would be more than just a revealer of a redemptive message. He would certainly be more than a moral example to follow as humans trudge their way up the stairway to heaven. This kind of God has no problem coming down and joining the human race, so the divine savior could become a man. Since this savior is an actual human being—the ultimate human being, in fact—he is capable of joining alienated humans to himself, taking them into his bosom like little matchsticks absorbed into a blazing bonfire. But equally important: Since this savior is also fully divine, he is able to take those absorbed people not partway but *all the way* back to the God he came from.

These, then, are the issues that drove the ancient debates about the Trinity. They weren't just abstractions from human philosophy (though some ideas borrowed from Greek philosophy were deemed useful, as we will see). But the key point is that there's nothing abstract about the Trinity. It's not an *idea* but a real-world *promise*. The things you say—or anyone says—about the Trinity will determine how that person tries to find the afterlife. Nothing could be more relevant, more important, more eternally significant than that.

"What must I do to be saved?" asked the terrified Philippian jailer. When Paul urged him to confess the name of the Lord Jesus—using the very same word by which the Greek Old Testament designated the LORD God—he was making a Trinitarian statement, even if no one had yet coined that term to describe it. The doctrine of the Trinity isn't theological trivia. It's nothing less than the proclamation of how to find eternal life.

So as you delve into this vital doctrine in the pages ahead, here's how the structure will unfold. Since the core of this book is about the Nicene Creed, we'll begin with a basic introduction that explains what creeds are, how they function, and why they're still important today. With that foundation in place, we'll be ready to explore four major topics related to the doctrine of God.

The first is "The Emergence of Old Testament Monotheism." In this section, we'll look at how the Israelites developed belief in one God against a polytheistic background. Our second topic is "Jesus: Fully God and Fully Man." Obviously, this section will deal with how Jesus came to be worshiped as divine within the context of Israel's historic confession of only one God. Next, we will explore "Nicene Christianity." As the early Christians grappled with how their received Jewish monotheism was supposed to relate to the worship of Jesus—along with the Holy Spirit—vigorous debates racked the ancient church. Only the convocation of the great council at Nicaea in 325 could solve the problem. Yet as we will see, the debate raged on for a few more decades before finally reaching a resolution. Our final section is "The Legacy of Nicaea." We'll finish the book with an exploration of how the Nicene Creed has impacted later Christian thinking about the Trinity, all the way to the present day. And to round it all out, we'll take a concluding look at how the doctrine of the Trinity expresses the gospel itself.

Are you ready to begin? Don't worry; this won't be a dry theological discourse that's way over your head. Instead, in a step-by-step fashion, we'll see how God has gradually revealed himself as a community of persons who eternally love one another, and who pour out their infinite love on the human race. To know God is to be invited into a community of perfect harmony and everlasting life. Who could ask for anything better than that?

1

What Is a Creed?

In the central region of the state of Wisconsin, a certain hilly area known as the Wisconsin Dells has become a tourist destination because of its scenic beauty. Since I lived in the Midwest for two decades, I can certainly understand the desire of my fellow flatlanders to see something other than drab prairie. Any kind of elevated terrain seems as beautiful as the Alps!

Among the many quirky tourist attractions in this area, one of the most popular is riding on the Wisconsin Ducks. These amphibious vehicles can navigate through lakes and rivers like boats, then roll out of the water to drive on paved roads. The overly enthusiastic marketing copy from the local tourism web page exclaims: "The CLASSIC DUCK TOUR splashes into the WISCONSIN RIVER and LAKE DELTON, climbs over SAND BARS, traverses over four miles of EXCLUSIVE SCENIC WILDERNESS TRAILS, and has been thrilling passengers for 75 YEARS and counting, ride THE ORIGINAL!"[1]

Just like a duck with waterproof feathers and webbed feet, these repurposed World War II vehicles can function on land or in water. After churning through the waves, they can emerge, dripping wet, for alternate use on dry ground.

Believe it or not, ancient church creeds have the same amphibious character as the Wisconsin Ducks. We tend to think of creeds as dry

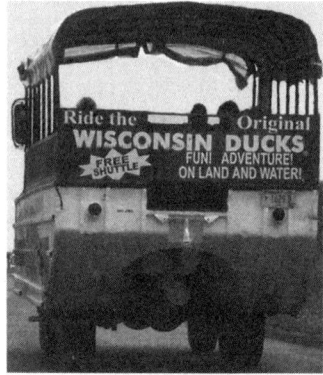

Wisconsin Dells Ducks (Wikimedia Commons, CC BY-SA 2.5).

things—formal words recited in churches with no water in sight. Churches that use creeds typically print the text in the bulletin or flash it on the screen for corporate reading. But ancient church creeds weren't originally meant for the Sunday service. Before they rolled into the pews, they swam in the sea: Creeds were intended to be recited during baptism.

Christian, What Do You Believe?

During the ancient church era (that is, from the time of the apostles until about four hundred years after them), getting everyone to believe the right theology was a real challenge. Lots of heresies—false views about God and Jesus—spread rapidly across the Roman Empire. One heresy claimed the God of Israel was foolish and Jesus had come to proclaim an unknown, better God (Marcionism). Another heresy said salvation didn't come from Jesus on the cross but through mysterious secrets whispered to the special few (gnosticism). Yet another heresy claimed that Jesus didn't have a real, physical body, but was more like a ghost who only seemed human

22

(Docetism). Lots of people wanted to believe in Jesus. The problem was knowing what to believe!

That's where creeds came in. When people got baptized into true, biblical churches, the leaders made sure all the converts knew exactly what they were accepting. Of course, many ancient people couldn't read very well, if at all. Books were so expensive that most people couldn't own them. Instead of learning correct theology through private reading, the converts of the ancient church were given pastoral instruction for several weeks (sometimes even for several years) prior to their baptism. This time of focused learning was called *catechesis*, from the Greek word for teaching.

A major assignment during the prebaptismal class was to memorize a creed. These words were said to be "handed out" by the instructor, then "given back" to the bishop when the convert went down into the water. The recitation of the creed wasn't a final exam from a doctrine class. It was more than just head knowledge. Instead, the baptized person was shifting stories—changing from one narrative about the world to a vastly different one. The converts of those days had been born into paganism and were steeped in Greco-Roman mythology. The deeds of Jupiter, Apollo, Venus, and a horde of other deities had shaped the person's world.

But now, the new believer was switching to the biblical narrative of Israel's God, a story that reached its high point in Jesus Christ and would surely culminate with his return for judgment and rewards. Creeds were memorized in catechesis and recited in the water so the convert would have a brief, handy summary of the new story they were joining.

This was why ancient baptisms always included exorcism. The old gods had to be washed away so the Holy Spirit could take up residence in the believer. This was also why ancient baptisms were performed in the nude. Everything from the

Baptismal font in Sbeitla, Tunisia. Photo by Agnieszka Wolska (Wikimedia Commons, CC BY-SA 3.0).

past was left behind. "If anyone is in Christ, he is a new creation. The old has passed away; behold, the new has come" (2 Cor. 5:17). When the baptized person came up from the opposite end of the pool from where they entered, they received a white robe that signified being clothed in Christ. They also drank a mixture of milk and honey—for like the Israelites of the exodus, they had just passed through water and arrived in the promised land. Eventually, the baptismal pools were set inside octagonal buildings next to the church. Why eight sides? Because seven was the number of completion, so eight represented the first step into newness of life.

Creeds, then, were more than just doctrinal summaries. They were short stories that served as abridgments of a longer tale. They articulated the creative work of God, the mighty deeds of his Son, the coming of the Spirit in the church, and the Christian's hope at the end of the age. This was a glorious new narrative to replace the decrepit myths of the gods.

The Origin of Creeds

Some people might think that reciting creeds is unbiblical. "Where in Scripture are we commanded to do that?" a critic might ask. In this view, creeds must have crept into church history after the time of the first-century apostles.

Not at all. Creeds were part of Christian worship right from the beginning. Jewish synagogue worship included many recitations of blessings and prayer formulas. The earliest Christians, who were Jews, kept this practice going and added new truths about Jesus to their verbal professions about the one, true God.

Creeds are entirely biblical. In fact, several creeds are quoted in the New Testament. One of the most prominent appears in 1 Corinthians 15. The apostle Paul says, "For I delivered to you as of first importance what I also received: that Christ died for our sins in accordance with the Scriptures, that he was buried, that he was raised on the third day in accordance with the Scriptures" (vv. 3–4). Notice that Paul says he "received" these words. After his dramatic conversion on the road to Damascus, the Jerusalem church taught him this formula, which has a creedal structure in the original Greek. These words come from the 30s, immediately after Paul's conversion, making them earlier than any of the Gospels, Epistles, or other New Testament books. What we have here is the primordial confession of the ancient church!

The central idea of these earliest, most primitive creeds is "Jesus is Lord." This is a kind of stock Christian saying, a fixed expression that signals belief in Jesus's resurrection. Paul tells us in Romans 10:9 that "if you confess with your mouth that Jesus is Lord and believe in your heart that God raised him from the dead, you will be saved." Notice that for Paul, inner belief of the heart wasn't enough. He told the Romans to believe, then to confess their beliefs out loud.

The word "confess" is an important creedal term. In Greek, it is *homologeo*, which means to be one-minded, or more literally, to "say the same word." When we confess a creed aloud, we are "same-saying" the words that other believers accept as well. What a beautiful picture of church unity! On Sunday morning, creeds articulate the truths that countless believers through the ages have likewise professed, and which fellow Christians around the world are also proclaiming on that day. Or when a creed is recited in the waters of baptism, each new believer, no matter their background, is embracing the same core truths about the mighty work of God. Verbal confession of creeds expresses the unity of the universal church.

Creeds, then, emerge directly from God's Word. In addition to the examples given above, brief creeds that emphasize the lordship of Jesus appear in Acts 8:37; Romans 1:3–4, 4:24, and 8:34; 1 Corinthians 8:6; Philippians 2:6–11; and 1 Timothy 2:5–6 and 3:16.

What happened next? Over the coming decades, the ancient Christians expanded the simple New Testament formulas so the words memorized and recited in baptism would more fully explain the new story being embraced. Some defenders of the faith also realized that these brief summaries of Christianity could be used to refute heretics, who told a countermyth to the authentic Chistian story. Creeds could also guard against erroneous Bible interpretation. No preacher should ever claim to find concepts in Scripture that contradict the central storyline about the Creator and his Christ. In all these ways, creeds helped the early church hone its understanding of sound doctrine.

Creedal Terminology

By the second century AD, the ancient Christians had begun to call their creeds a "rule." They used terms like "rule of faith," "rule of truth," or "ecclesiastical rule." The rule of faith (*regula fidei*) wasn't superior to Scripture. Nobody thought it came directly from God like the Bible. Instead, it was viewed as a widely agreed-upon (and therefore accurate) synopsis of Scripture's main ideas. Although the rule of faith didn't have the exact same wording in every church, its flow of ideas followed similar lines. The various expressions tended to have a lot of verbal overlap in the congregations where they were being used.

In addition to "rule," the ancient Christians also used the term "symbol." The Greek word *sumbolon*, like the Latin equivalent *symbolum*, originally referred to a little token which was broken in half so that the two parties making a contract would each have a sign of what had been agreed upon. From this came the idea (as the English word "symbol" means today) of an outward expression of an intangible idea. Modern symbols can be physical, like the Nike swoosh or the Golden Arches of McDonald's, but they can also be verbal. When we hear "Just do it," we think of athletic gear. When we hear "I'm lovin' it," we think of burgers. Likewise, an ancient creed was a verbal symbol that represented timeless truths. The early Christians could hear these audible words that stood for lofty theological concepts. In a sense, by pledging themselves to this creed, they were making a sacred contract with God and each other. Furthermore, a *sumbolon* was something secret that allowed authentic participants to perceive meanings that no one else could understand. This was useful in an age of Christian persecution.

The word "creed" comes from the Latin word *credo*, meaning "I believe." *Credo* was typically the first word of a creed, designating the theological content to be confessed: "I believe in God the Father Almighty," and so on. Sometimes, a plural form was used instead: "We believe." Either way, the main purpose of a creed was to articulate *credenda*, the doctrines to be believed.

Movement Toward Precision

Over time, the various versions of the rule of faith began to crystallize into fixed, standardized creeds that were intended to have verbal precision. The baptismal creed used at Rome in the fourth century AD was called the Old Roman Symbol. It was authoritative throughout much of Italy, while Africa, Gaul, Spain, and Britain developed their own similar creeds. Egypt, Antioch, and Jerusalem had baptismal creeds as well. Most scholars see significant continuity between the Old Roman Symbol and the creed most often recited in Western churches today, the Apostles' Creed.

Did this creed really come from the apostles? One ancient commentator, Rufinus of Aquileia, tells us that after Jesus ascended back to heaven, the twelve apostles got together and wrote up this short summary of the gospel, each one contributing a clause as he saw fit. Modern scholars view that story as legend.

Although it's true that the ideas found in this creed are apostolic in the sense that they trace back to the time of the New Testament, the Latin text itself dates to the 700s. It comes from the pen of Saint Pirmin, a Spanish missionary to the pagan Germans who were slowly being evangelized. Around 813, the Frankish emperor Charlemagne required all Christians in his realm to use the Apostles' Creed as their standard. Ever since then, it has been the most popular creed among churches that have European roots. Eventually, the Latin text was translated into German and used widely by the Lutherans. English translations were also made by the Church of England for the *Book of Common Prayer*. Today, some American churches recite this version or another one close to it.

But what about the Nicene Creed—the subject of this book? We might say that the origins of this creed are less broad and organic than other creedal formulas. Unlike those that morphed over centuries of pastoral usage, the Nicene Creed emerged at a precise time: the council about the Trinity in 325, which you will soon be hearing more about. Church historians debate whether an earlier baptismal creed was used as its basis or it was written from scratch for that occasion. In either case, the Nicene Creed can be pegged to a specific moment in history in a way that many others cannot.

Roots of Trinitarianism

Before we can get to that pivotal moment, we need to set the stage. Trinitarianism wasn't invented by Christians in the fourth century AD. It was the fruit of centuries-long reflection about how to properly affirm the deity of Christ alongside God the Father. Of course, the story of the Trinity didn't begin with the arrival of Jesus on earth. The Old Testament had already shown that the God who sat enthroned in heaven nevertheless had personal aspects of his being that went forth and impacted the world. God's oneness had to be extended into multiplicity, or he would be irrelevant to humankind, a remote king on a distant throne. Fortunately for us, the God of the Bible does extend himself into the world. Those extensions are part of his own being, yet somehow they differ from he who remains in heaven. The Trinity was an Old Testament concept that got more fully expressed in the New.

To ancient people, however, the multiplicity of God wasn't the most surprising thing about him. Pagan gods often came in triads, so threeness within the divine realm was an easy idea to embrace. The real challenge was to accept what the earliest Hebrews confessed in their own creed-like way: "Hear, O Israel: The LORD our God, the LORD is one"

29

(Deut. 6:4). To really understand the Trinity, we first have to get our minds around the subject of our next chapter: the universal human belief that the world abounds with innumerable gods. Only then can we appreciate the astonishing, incredible, and counterintuitive notion of Hebrew monotheism—that the "LORD is one."

Part 1

The Emergence
of Old Testament
Monotheism

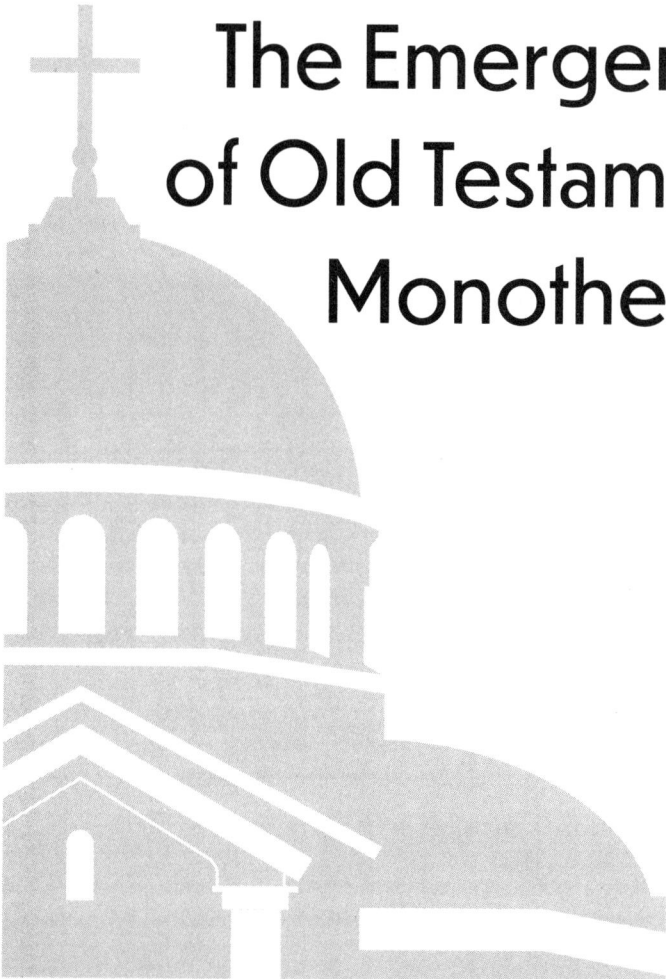

2

Out of Nature, Many Gods

I n a book about God, it's worth asking at the outset, "Why would people believe in deities at all?" Anthropologists, those brave people who study human behavior in all its noble and unsavory forms, typically don't agree on much, but they do agree on this: Religion is inherent to our species. In every time, place, and culture, people have worshiped entities beyond the natural world. Humans are truly *homo religiosus*: a worshiping being.

This isn't to say that every single person will worship a god. A few people identify as atheists—people with no outward religion or belief in the divine. Yet anthropologists will tell you that atheism is a relatively recent phenomenon and isn't widespread. Among all the humans who have ever walked this planet, only a tiny fraction have been total unbelievers. And even atheists engage in inborn religious behavior, applying worship-like beliefs, practices, and rituals to their supposedly secular lives. It's as if they are hard-wired to worship even though they claim to despise it.

Unlike every other animal, something drives our species to contemplate a world beyond our senses. We believe in another realm inhabited by sentient beings with extraordinary power. Typically, these beings are much like humans, yet endowed with capabilities we don't have. They might not all act the same way, demand the same things, or even demand anything at all. Their names across the ages are innumerable. Yet people everywhere have believed in them, considering them "gods," "spirits," "fairies," "ghosts," or "ancestors." Always, we have tried to get on their good side and avoid their malice. Where did this ubiquitous human tendency come from?

Seeking the Origin of Religion

French anthropologist Pascal Boyer, now teaching in America, has spent his career examining the innate religious impulse of human beings. In his book *Religion Explained: The Evolutionary Origins of Religious Thought*, he lays out four common theories about why humans started to worship.[1]

First, religion offered causation for natural events that primitive humans couldn't explain. Deities must be behind the mysteries of thunderstorms, tsunamis, and earthquakes. Second, religion comforted our ancestors with the hope of an afterlife, the chance that maybe death wasn't actually the end of all things. Third, religion provided social order and perpetuated morality. It served as an effective glue to help communities collect resources and dispense them with a minimum of friction. Fourth, religion was a mental impairment, a flaw in humanity's ability to reason. People are just naturally gullible and superstitious. They think the number seven is lucky while thirteen is not. Why? No reason; people just believe it. Religion arose as a large-scale superstition whose absurdities were easier to go along with than refute.

All of these theories, Boyer believes, contain elements of truth but don't tell the real story. For Boyer, evolutionary biology is the true answer (as the name of his book implies). People don't "choose" to adopt religions so they can meet a social or psychological need. Rather, religion inevitably emerges from the way the human brain evolved. Our distant past as either predators or prey made us deeply aware of the unseen world. We became inclined to notice any rustlings in the grass as a possible active agent. If it turned out to be just the wind, we dismissed it without any real cost to us. But if it was a gazelle, we just found our next meal, enabling us to live another day. Or if it was a lion, we detected it and escaped in time. Either way, we benefited. For the sake of hunter-gatherer survival, our species became acutely aware of unseen forces lurking around us.

These forces especially mattered to us if they were human; that is, a friend or foe with the same sophisticated mental apparatus we have. An enemy with a spear would be a far more intelligent adversary than a lion, so we'd do well to suspect someone malicious might be nearby. An ally, on the other hand, might have valuable knowledge, so it was worth considering that possibility as well. Maybe we could tap into their insights and thrive.

People without these suspicious instincts died prematurely. The lion or the enemy spearman got them. The more vigilant survivors passed on the genes that made their offspring look for human-type agents everywhere. As anthropologist Stewart Guthrie puts it, we tend to see "faces in the clouds" (the title of his book) because we're strongly inclined to imagine humanoid beings everywhere. We so naturally expect them—in fact, we *want* to find them—that we end up projecting them onto the shadowy, hidden corners of our world. The fully developed set of behaviors that emerged from this instinct is what came to be called religion.

To drive home this point, let's consider the ideas of yet another scientist, this time from the field of psychology. Justin L. Barrett is the author of *Why Would Anyone Believe in God?*, which is precisely the question we're asking in this chapter.[2] Barrett shows again and again that evolutionary biology has conditioned humans to believe in gods, ghosts, spirits, and other humanoid supernatural entities. An all-powerful, all-knowing type of god is especially meaningful to us. Such a being would be a supreme ally if we pleased him, or a dreadful enemy if we did not. By the end of his book, Barrett has so proven his point about our innate religious impulses that he has changed his question to "Why would anyone *not* believe in God?"

Much like Boyer, Barrett points to the brain's ADD—its agency detection device. This is the part of the brain that, when considering a sense impression, tries to determine whether active agency is behind it. Did some living creature cause the impression or event? If not, we can dismiss it and go on our way. But if an agent was involved, our speedy recognition might help us gain a benefit (a friend's information) or avoid a threat (being preyed upon).

Because the brain's ADD was so useful to our primitive ancestors, it became what Barrett calls a HADD: a *hypersensitive* agency detection device. This hypersensitivity to possible causal agents led, in turn, to widespread belief in gods or spirits. We found agents everywhere, then described them, told stories about them, and started giving them names. Soon, other people in our village agreed with our patterns of discernment. Beliefs about gods became systematized and regulated. In this way, religion was born—an entirely logical outcome for hypersensitive people trying to survive in a dangerous world. Nothing could be more natural for human beings than to worship.

The Truth of Polytheism

Though secular anthropology can offer some helpful ideas about the human religious impulse, it completely misses the actual explanation because that explanation doesn't come from a scientific worldview. The most basic reason why everyone, everywhere, has believed in gods isn't that it conferred survival advantages on the human race. While that might provide part of the story, at the heart of the matter, religion didn't arise from evolution. Nor did it arise from the inner structure of the human mind. It arose from the nature of reality itself. People believed in gods because *gods actually exist*, just as surely as the trees, clouds, rocks, and animals that we see around us.

This may sound strange to the ears of twenty-first-century Westerners. Modern people like us have a hard time believing what many cultures have accepted without question: Invisible spirits—sometimes cooperative, sometimes malevolent—are a fact of life. Yet we are the exception. For the majority of humanity, no special faith commitment was (or is) needed for gods, ghosts, and ancestral spirits. They are just part of the world. Of course they exist, just like visible things exist. Gods are part of what *is*, invariably and indubitably. Their presence is as undeniable as the blue sky above. Almost all human beings have thought this way.

But what about the original people of the biblical God—the ancient Israelites? Did they think this way? More importantly, do the inspired Scriptures tell us we ought to think this way? For a Christian, it is more important to determine what the Bible teaches than what some tribal shaman might have told his village. We want a biblical worldview, not a primitive one, even if that primitive one is incredibly widespread.

Perhaps surprisingly, Scripture does indeed teach the existence of other gods. Yet alongside this teaching comes the affirmation that Yahweh, the God of the Israelites, outranks them all. Other nations might cling to their weak deities, but the Israelites were supposed to worship only the all-powerful Lord. By the time of Jesus's arrival on earth, the Jews were fully committed to monotheism: the belief that there is one and only one God. But these seem like conflicting messages. Is there one God or many? How are we to make sense of what the Bible teaches?

Before we can get our minds around biblical monotheism, we must first recognize the essential truth of polytheism—that many gods actually do exist. As I said above, human religion arose not from evolution but from the nature of reality itself. People worship gods because there really are gods out there who want to receive human adoration.

Was the storm god Baal just the fantasy of the ancient Mesopotamians? Were the twelve Olympians the crazy invention of Greek mythmakers like Homer? Was the benevolent, protective god Vishnu just wishful thinking among ancient Hindus? Not at all. Those beings actually existed, along with many others. They accepted the names people gave them because that was a way to gain worship. Over time, the names faded but the beings did not. They still exist today. If some of them once empowered wicked leaders of the past, perhaps those same spirits are now active in the leadership of Iran or North Korea. If they previously received child sacrifices, today they might lurk around abortion clinics. In no way did they disappear. Nor are they the figments of human imagination. These beings are what Scripture calls *demons*.

What the Pagans Sacrifice

Consider the clear teaching of the apostle Paul about these things. In 1 Corinthians 10, he had to address believers at Corinth who wanted to eat meat that came from pagan sacrifices. Today, we don't think of meat as something religious. People go to a grocery store, buy some beef or chicken in a Styrofoam container—almost forgetting it was once part of an animal—and eat it for dinner without any spiritual thoughts. But in ancient times, meat didn't come from everyday market stalls like fruit or bread. It had priestly origins when the butchered animal was devoted to idolatrous gods. Such meat might be sold in a separate market, then be eaten in an unbeliever's home or even be consumed at a temple as part of a ritual meal for the god. Could the Corinthian Christians participate in any of that?

The apostle is clear that the idols themselves are nothing. A believer in Jesus need not fear these lifeless carvings of wood or stone. Yet Paul provides two examples in which eating food certainly did create an intimate association with God. The Lord's Supper of bread and wine observed by the early Christians was a "participation" or sharing in Jesus's sacrificial work (vv. 16–17 NIV). Likewise, the feasts of ancient Israel made them participants in the holy sacrifices at the altar of the Jerusalem temple (v. 18). The historic Jewish practice was for the priests to receive a good cut of the animal, and then the rest of the meat (though not the blood or the fat) could be distributed for others to eat (Lev. 7:11–36).

Third century painting of an agape feast.

39

What about sacrifices to the pagan gods? Paul taught that while idols need not be feared because their true power is nothing (1 Cor. 10:19), eating sacrificial meat in a temple did indeed create a spiritual association with the deity to whom it was offered. The apostle was particularly emphatic when he warned the Corinthians, "What pagans sacrifice they offer to demons and not to God. I do not want you to be participants with demons. You cannot drink the cup of the Lord and the cup of demons. You cannot partake of the table of the Lord and the table of demons" (vv. 20–21).

Paul went on to say that engaging in this kind of worship might provoke God to jealousy (v. 22). It would be a direct violation of the first commandment: "You shall have no other gods before me. You shall not make for yourself a carved image, or any likeness of anything that is in heaven above, or that is in the earth beneath, or that is in the water under the earth. You shall not bow down to them or serve them, for I the LORD your God am a jealous God" (Exod. 20:3–5).

Do you see what Scripture is teaching? In both of these texts, one from the Old Testament and one from the New, other gods aren't denied as existent. Far from it! They are treated as real beings who could be worshiped, though they are actually evil demons. Paul had no doubts about this. He knew it on the basis of what Scripture had already declared about the apostasy of the Israelites: "They stirred [God] to jealousy with strange gods; with abominations they provoked him to anger. They sacrificed to demons that were no gods. . . . You were unmindful of the Rock that bore you, and you forgot the God who gave you birth" (Deut. 32:16–18).

A complete survey of biblical demonology is beyond the scope of this book. However, it suffices to say that Scripture teaches the true, actual existence of demons, which are previously good angels that fell away from their created state of blessedness. These beings are sometimes imprisoned in hell, but other times they roam the earth, causing destruction wherever they go and usurping God's rightful worship. If some deluded humans are willing to offer up worship, a spiritual being—or perhaps many—will certainly show up to receive it.

Polytheism, then, isn't some strange quirk of human existence. It is ubiquitous in all times and places, as every anthropologist knows. Those early religions might have conferred some survival benefits or psychological comforts to our ancestors. That was probably part of their appeal. But the main reason people long ago engaged in worship (and still do today) is because *gods are real*. The demons can hurt people, or they can be induced to share power in ways we crave. Humans know this at a core level of our being, even if most Westerners have learned to suppress it. There are many, many spirits in our world. They are incredibly powerful. That is why gods and world religions are an ever-present fact of life.

How, then, did the Israelites muster the courage to confront this universal polytheism with a seemingly ridiculous counter-story about Yahweh's uniqueness? How did they even think up such a radical idea, much less institutionalize it in their laws and systems of worship? As we will see in the next chapter, it was no easy task to establish monotheism. Quite often, the early Hebrews failed to worship the LORD alone. Even so, it was their stubborn insistence on the oneness of God that laid the foundations for the full-fledged doctrine of the Trinity.

3

Out of Many Gods, One Lord

Though God's people in the Old Testament (called the "Hebrews" or "Israelites" early on, then "Jews" at a later period) had many prayers, exclamations, and benedictions in their worship, they weren't creedal—that is, they didn't typically recite confessions of doctrine like Christians. Even so, the Jews had at least one formal statement that approached the nature of a creed. It was a succinct verbal expression of the true faith, designed to protect God's people from worshiping false deities. This expression is known as the Shema because of its first words in Hebrew: "*Shema, Yisrael!*"—"Hear, O Israel!" The statement goes on to say, "The LORD our God, the LORD *is* one!" (Deut. 6:4 NKJV).

We can think of this little statement as a kind of Hebrew creed that confesses monotheism. In the massive tome *Creeds and Confessions of Faith in the Christian Tradition* by scholars Jaroslav Pelikan and Valerie Hotchkiss, the Shema is the only Old Testament text cited in eight hundred pages of creedal examples. Yet the Shema's primordial words stand behind all other creeds. Pelikan and Hotchkiss say, "This expression of faith could be called the 'creed' of Judaism. Observant Jewish males recite it every morning and evening . . . [It] should be the first prayer a child learns and the last prayer on a dying person's lips."[1] In other words, the Shema expresses the most fundamental thing about the nature of God: his oneness. No wonder Jesus identified it as the first and foremost commandment (Mark 12:29)!

Yet as we consider the Shema's relationship to monotheism, let's notice a few important things about it. First, the statement doesn't say there are no other gods. It asserts only that Israel should be devoted to "our God"—the God who was leading the people into the promised land. Nothing is said about whether other gods exist, only that the Hebrews should have just one. However, in the previous chapter of Deuteronomy when God gave Moses the Ten Commandments, the first commandment specifically mentioned the existence of other gods but said the Hebrews shouldn't worship any of them. Often, that verse is translated, "You shall have no other gods before me" (Deut. 5:7). Yet other translations say, "no other gods *besides* me." Clearly, other gods existed; but Israel was supposed to reject them.

The second important thing about the Shema is how God is named. Two words for God are used. The first is typically written with small capitals in English Bibles: "the LORD." This designation means the original Hebrew word consisted of four letters known as the Tetragrammaton: *yod, heh, vav, heh*, or YHWH. Since the ancient Jews refused to utter this word lest they accidentally blaspheme, we do not know the proper sound of it. Modern scholars assume it was something like Yahweh. Instead of printing this holy name, today's Bible versions usually just put "the LORD." This reflects the term that the Jews substituted whenever they came across this unsayable word while reading the biblical text aloud: "Adonai," the normal term for "lord."

Yet the Shema uses a second word to name the singular divine being: "God." Here, the original Hebrew word was *Elohim*. This is a pluralized (and thus majestic) form of the word *El*. In the religious pantheons of many ancient Semitic peoples such as the Canaanites, El was the supreme deity with fatherly attributes. But this name took on special meaning for the Hebrews when Jacob, the grandson of Abraham, received a new name. God told him, "Your name shall no longer be called Jacob, but Israel, for you have striven with God and with men, and have prevailed" (Gen. 32:28). The word *Isra-el* means "he strives with God," or maybe "God strives." Either way, it reveals that Jacob/Israel, whose twelve sons founded the famous twelve tribes, had wrestled with the God known as El, or as he is often called in Scripture, Elohim.

So which is it—Elohim or Yahweh? Are they the same being? Did the ancient Hebrews worship two different Gods? Is the Canaanite El the same as Israel's Elohim? And what about all those other deities who provided such a strong religious temptation to the Israelites, such as Baal or Asherah? Did those beings exist alongside God and vie with him for supremacy?

The answer is no. The Israelites worshiped the one and only God. Yet too often, they messed up and worshiped demonic entities as well. The process of extricating the true God out of the polytheistic cultures around Israel took time and hit a lot of speed bumps along the way. Let's take a closer look at exactly how it happened.

Henotheism Versus Monotheism

A fair assessment of the entire Old Testament reveals that the earliest Hebrews functioned with what is called *henotheism*. Only later did the returnees from the Babylonian exile—that is, the Jews of Judaea—develop a robust commitment to actual *monotheism*. What is the difference between the two?

These are both Greek-based terms, so we need to examine their etymology. Each of them combines the word for belief in a deity ("theism") with a Greek word for "one," though with slightly different nuances. *Henos* means "one" in the sense of "this one, as opposed to another." If I select a crayon out of a box and start to color with it, I am using *henos* crayon—this particular one out of many possibilities. In contrast, *monos* has the idea of uniqueness or singularity. How many Statues of Liberty are in New York? How many Eiffel Towers are in Paris? How many Big Bens are in London? In each case, there is *monos* of these—one and only one.

The Old Testament contains many henotheistic statements. Consider the passage in Exodus that describes the terrible night of the Passover when God judged the Egyptians by slaying their firstborn sons. In addition to the humans who fell under his curse, God also declared, "I will bring judgment on all the gods of Egypt" (12:12 NIV). Clearly, those gods existed and were there to be judged.

Lest you think that curse was spoken metaphorically about nonexistent deities represented by fake idols, recall what Moses sang in victory after the Israelites escaped from Egypt: "Who is like you, O Lord, among the gods? Who is like you, majestic in holiness, awesome in glorious deeds, doing wonders?" (Exod. 15:11). In other words, God is the greatest of many deities.

A bit later, we hear the joyful words of Jethro, Moses's father-in-law and an original worshiper of Yahweh. He exclaimed, "Blessed be the Lord, who has delivered you out of the hand of the Egyptians and out of the hand of Pharaoh and has delivered the people from under the hand of the Egyptians. Now I know that the Lord is greater than all gods" (Exod. 18:10–11). Such examples could be multiplied many times over. Israel's one God is said to be more powerful than the many other deities which do exist but are vastly inferior. As we saw in the last chapter, they are actually fallen angels, or demons (Lev. 17:7; Deut. 32:16–17).

Alongside these henotheistic ideas, we see an increasing drive toward a more robust monotheism. The closer the heathen gods are investigated, the more impotent they are discovered to be. Eventually, the Israelites came to realize that they can't even be dignified with the name "gods." They are so empty, so false, so lacking in power that God's people can essentially view them as nonexistent. One God rules over all the earth. He stands alone. He is supreme. He isn't just for Israel, but for all nations. The horde of demonic powers, which are personified by idols, can be considered as non-gods.

We see this idea occasionally in the Psalms. For example, in Psalm 86:8, King David proclaimed, "There is none like you among the gods, O Lord, nor are there any works like yours." This is a henotheistic statement. But in verse 10, David went further, declaring, "You are great and do wondrous things; you alone are God." Now there is monotheism! Ancient Israel's greatest king repeated this claim after God made a special covenant with him, known as the Davidic covenant. "You are great, O Lord God. For there is none like you, and there is no God besides you, according to all that we have heard with our ears" (2 Sam. 7:22). Since David knew God intimately, he had begun to understand God's absolute uniqueness in the world.

The prophets of Israel took up this idea even more clearly. Yahweh wasn't just for Israel but controlled all the nations. He could use foreign kingdoms to chastise his people if they didn't worship him alone. He could also bring down those wicked nations whenever he wished. The heathen gods, personified by dumb idols, are nothing. "Can man make for himself gods? Such are not gods!" the prophet Jeremiah exclaimed (Jer. 16:20).

Likewise, Isaiah mocked the gold and silver idols of the pagans, which they insanely worshiped. Such fools "hire a goldsmith, and he makes it into a god; then they fall down and worship! They lift it to their shoulders, they carry it, they set it in its place, and it stands there; it cannot move from its place. If one cries to it, it does not answer or save him from his trouble" (Isa. 46:6–7). Only Israel's God is the true God; only he can save. A common statement recorded by the prophets is "I am the LORD, and there is no other" (Isa. 44:6; 45:5–6, 18, 21–22; 46:9; Joel 2:27). By the time the Old Testament era came to a close, this idea was securely established.

Why did God's people move from polytheism to henotheism to monotheism (not in a straight line, though they eventually got there)? One answer is obvious: because God's clear revelation of his own singularity caused his people to realize this truth. Surely that was part of it. God is actually monotheistic, not henotheistic, and his people finally discerned the full biblical teaching.

What else might have contributed to the Israelites' spiritual understanding? Perhaps it was because they were originally desert dwellers, a people awed by the vastness of the stars at night. A supreme being must have made such a breathtaking cosmos, they reasoned. Or perhaps it was God's covenant faithfulness (his loyal love, or *hesed*) experienced by Abraham, Joseph, the refugees of the exodus, or David. Such a great and merciful God must stand alone. These ideas no doubt lent themselves to monotheistic conceptions.

In any case, one thing was certain about Israel's God: He wasn't going to remain aloof from the world. Though he reigned from a throne in the sky with radiant splendor, he also cared about the earthly sphere. He (and only he) had created it down to its finest detail, so he wasn't about to abandon it. A benevolent and almighty God would certainly interact with his world and the people in it.

Yet how could he do that and still be enthroned on high? The ancient Israelites thought of Yahweh or Elohim as seated on a throne not far above the face of the earth. A solid blue dome overhead contained the sun, moon, and stars. It was known as the *raqia*, or firmament. Above this firm canopy, which was taut like a tent or perhaps hard like bronze (Job 37:18; Ps. 19:4; Isa. 40:22), was an ocean of fresh water which sometimes fell through the "floodgates of the heavens" as rain (Gen. 8:2 NIV; Ps. 148:3–4). Yet Yahweh had laid beams across this watery expanse to support his heavenly temple

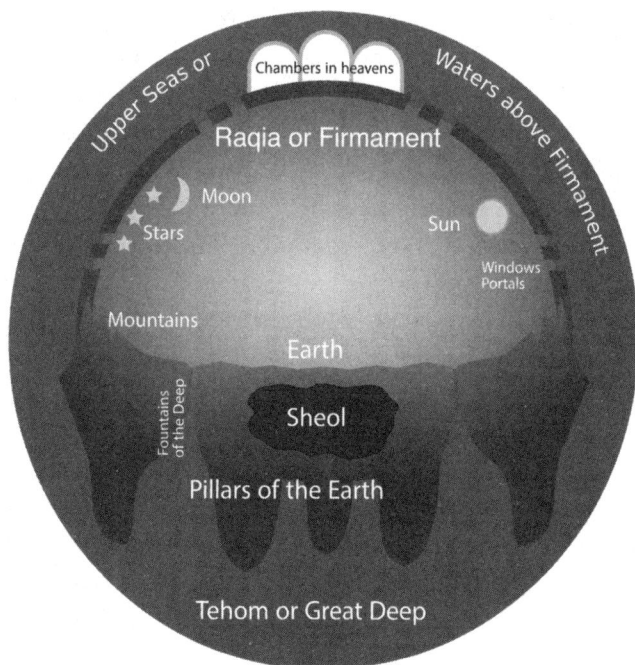

Early Hebrew conception of the universe. Image by Tom Lemmens (Wikimedia Commons, CC BY 4.0).

49

(Pss. 29:10; 104:3). God's throne sat in that temple and his feet rested on the dome, which was blue like sapphire (Exod. 24:10). "This is what the LORD says: 'Heaven is my throne, and the earth is my footstool'" (Isa. 66:1 NIV). By what means could this glorious God above send forth his power to the earth below without leaving his heavenly home?

Word and Breath

Psalm 33:6 is the most Trinitarian verse in the Old Testament; it declares, "By the word of the LORD the heavens were made, and by the breath of his mouth all their host." In other words, when Yahweh wished to make the cosmos, he did so via two entities: his Word and his Breath. The Hebrew term *dabar* means a spoken word, while *ruach* means "breath, wind, or spirit." These two entities are how God shapes the world. Isn't this exactly what Genesis 1 revealed right at the beginning of the Bible? The Holy Spirit was hovering over the chaotic waters until Yahweh uttered his verbal command, "*Yehi!* Let there be!" Here we see that God's Word and Breath worked together as his formative powers to shape the earth. The ancient Israelites understood that their one God extended himself into the world through his speaking and his exhalation. Let's consider each of these concepts in turn.

A word is something that exists in a mind until it goes forth with impact. Though it always belongs to the speaker, it is sent out to do something. As I sit here at my desk, I can conceptualize a word in my mind. Of course, it cannot affect anyone until I utter it. But when I do, the hearer is impacted, for better or worse. If I say "pizza" or "puppy," the hearer is affected positively. But if I say "scab" or "cockroach," the effect will be negative. Either way, the word that sits in my mind does nothing. Only after it is uttered does it make an impact. Though I remain in my place, I send forth my word to accomplish an action. This is what's known as a speech-act. Words *do* things.

The same is true of one's "breath." It is one's own, for it is exhaled from within. Yet it does things in the world. We can blow kisses or emit the stink of garlic, both of which power-fully affect the recipient. Consider a naughty child who leans over a sibling's birthday cake and blows out the candles—that will make a big impact! Everyone knows whose breath did the rascally deed, for the breath belongs to the breather.

In the same way, God's Breath is invisible yet powerful. This is especially true when we think of it as wind. A hurri-cane or tornado can wreak havoc wherever it rages. Or a gen-tle breeze can refresh the weary traveler. A prevailing wind can have a formative effect over time, bending mighty trees before its constant, steady blowing. According to Scripture, the divine Breath goes out from God and accomplishes great things. Moses understood this after the Israelites crossed the Red Sea on dry land. "I will sing to the LORD," he said, "for he has triumphed gloriously; the horse and his rider he has thrown into the sea. . . . At the blast of your nostrils the waters piled up; the floods stood up in a heap. . . . You blew with your wind [*ruach*]; the sea covered them; they sank like lead in the mighty waters" (Exod. 15:1, 8, 10). God didn't have to send angels to fight against Pharaoh. All he had to do was exhale.

Extensions of the One God

From beginning to end, the Old Testament teaches the exis-tence of God's powerful Word and Breath. These concepts don't undercut the Shema, nor do they deny monotheism. They only extend divine power from the heavenly throne into all realms of human existence.

51

Scripture uses the Hebrew phrase "the word of the LORD" more than 240 times, usually to describe the sending of a prophetic message (Gen. 15:1; Deut. 5:5; Josh. 8:27; 2 Sam. 7:4; 1 Kings 13:20; Jer. 1:2; Ezek. 1:3). This message isn't just a verbal pronouncement but a personal and living entity that has power. For example, the Word can heal: "He sent out his word and healed them, and delivered them from their destruction" (Ps. 107:20). Or the Word hastens to carry out God's orders: "He sends out his command to the earth; his word runs swiftly" (Ps. 147:15). In fact, the Word is an obedient agent of the divine will: "So shall my word be that goes out from my mouth; it shall not return to me empty, but it shall accomplish that which I purpose, and shall succeed in the thing for which I sent it" (Isa. 55:11).

This same kind of personalization can be applied to the Breath of God. It is a dynamic agent that comes upon human beings to empower them for mighty deeds, such as when Samson slew a lion (Judg. 14:6) or Gideon called troops into battle (Judg. 6:34). The prophet Ezekiel considered the Spirit as the very "hand of God" upon him (3:14; 8:1–3; 37:1). When the Breath of the LORD blew across the earth for judgment, the people withered (Isa. 40:7). On the other hand, when God's Spirit descended in grace, wonderful gifts were bestowed: wisdom and understanding, counsel and might, knowledge and fear of the LORD (Isa. 11:2). Wherever the Breath of God went in the world, the fullness of God's presence came rushing in. And who was this being? He was *Ruach Ha-Kodesh*, the Holy Spirit. King David understood this truth when he pleaded from the depths of his sin, "Take not your Holy Spirit from me" (Ps. 51:11; see also Isa. 63:10).

The Trinity, then, isn't some alien Christian doctrine that was forced onto the Hebrew Scriptures by the early church fathers. Just the opposite: The ancient Christians clarified what was already latent in the Old Testament. But they didn't gain their insights primarily by conversing with Jewish rabbis (though that occasionally happened). First and foremost, they were guided by the revelation of Jesus Christ. The ancient church's experience of his life, death, and resurrection led them from the biblical depiction of Israel's LORD to the only possible outcome: a Father God who dwells with his Son and his Spirit at all times. The Old Testament set up this idea within its pages so that when Jesus came along, his true disciples would be ready to receive him as the Son of God.

4

Does Yahweh Have a Son?

Most people in America today know that Jesus is called the Son of God. One of our most popular Christmas carols exclaims, "Hark! The herald angels sing, 'Glory to the newborn King! Hail the heaven-born Prince of Peace! Hail the Son of Righteousness!'" Christmas cards often quote the words of Isaiah 9:6: "For to us a child is born, to us a son is given." The concept of God's Son coming into the world at Christmas is so common that we rarely stop to consider how strange it really is.

In the previous two chapters, we learned that polytheism has been a religious norm throughout humanity's existence. But over time, God's people developed a henotheism that eventually led to full-blown monotheism. So how did they make room for God's Son? Was that something the ancient Israelites believed? Was it part of their Scriptures? If Yahweh is one God, how could he have a Son without destroying the unity of monotheism?

We have already seen that the Old Testament depicted the extension of God's power into the world through his Word

The angel tells the shepherds that Jesus is born. Image from *The Story of the Bible from Genesis to Revelation in Simple Language for the Young*, 1873.

and his Breath. Those entities were sometimes "personalized" as concrete beings. Yet they weren't really considered sons, for they lacked the human features that a true son would have. In particular, they didn't have visible bodies. However, the Hebrew Scriptures describe other times when heavenly beings entered the world in humanoid form. Such appearances happened long before the baby Jesus was ever laid in a Bethlehem manger. Physical manifestations of God occurred throughout the Old Testament. Could any of these humanoids be considered the Son of God?

Notice that I said "humanoid," not "human." For now, let's only consider those beings that looked and acted like a person but really weren't. In other words, they weren't a full and complete man, 100 percent identical to everyone on earth. The word for God doing that is "incarnation," a coming "in the flesh." We must reserve this term for Jesus being born of Mary. But what about human-like appearances prior to the incarnation of Jesus? What do we call those? To describe this phenomenon, we use the term *theophany*, which means a visible manifestation of God in our world.

Old Testament Theophanies

Among the ancient Israelites, God was sometimes seen in nonhuman forms such as fire, clouds, or smoke. For example, the Hebrews in the wilderness were led by a pillar of cloud in the daytime and a pillar of fire at night (Exod. 13:21). When God came down to Mount Sinai, raging flames and billowing smoke enveloped the summit (Exod. 19:18). Thunder and lightning (Job 37:4) or storms and whirlwinds (Nah. 1:3) could also be visible manifestations of God.

Other times, God sent forth messengers in human form. Usually these messengers were what we call angels: powerful, glorious beings who serve God and protect his holiness. As the Creator of everything, Yahweh could be considered the "father" of these beings, which is why angels were sometimes referred to as the sons of God (Job 1:6). Biblical angels certainly weren't the eternal God himself, but timebound creatures whom he made long ago.

However, one of these beings, known as the angel of the LORD, often seemed to be something more than just a creature. He is treated like God in human form. Consider these biblical examples:

- In Genesis 16, the angel of the LORD appeared to Hagar, the handmaiden of Abraham. The angel gave her comfort and predicted the birth of her son, Ishmael. Hagar recognized that it was "the LORD who spoke to her" (v. 13).

- In Genesis 18, three "men" appeared to Abraham at the oaks of Mamre, where he entertained them graciously. One of the visitors, who predicted Abraham would bear a son, is called "the LORD" (vv. 1–2, 10).

- In Exodus 3, Moses encountered the angel of the LORD inside a burning bush. From within the bush, which did not burn up, the angel called to Moses and told him to remove his sandals, for he was standing on holy ground. The speaker identified himself as God (vv. 4–6).

- In Judges 13, Samson's mother was told by the angel of the LORD that she would bear a son who would deliver Israel from oppression. Her husband was terrified, for he knew that he and his wife had seen God (v. 22).

In each of these examples, the angel wasn't just *sent from* God like a normal angel would be. He was *equated with* God. This shows that God can sometimes assume a form which appears to the human eye like a person, having a recognizable face and body. Typically (though not always), the

Hagar and the Angel by Giuseppe Bottani, ca. 1776.

theophany displays heightened glory and splendor. Nevertheless, the glory is diminished enough so people can survive the encounter, which wouldn't be the case if the full glory of God's face were revealed (Exod. 33:20).

Where else does the Bible describe humanoid appearances of God? In our previous chapter, we briefly mentioned one of the most intriguing stories in all of Scripture. It is the story of Jacob, the grandson of Abraham, who wrestled with a "man" through a whole night (Gen. 32:22–32). Just as dawn was breaking, the mysterious wrestler realized Jacob wouldn't quit, so he touched his hip and threw it out of socket. The wrestler then renamed Jacob as Israel because he had "striven with God and with men, and [had] prevailed" (v. 28). Amazed by what he had experienced, the newly renamed Israel concluded, "I have seen God face to face, and yet my life has been delivered" (v. 30). Clearly, the divine wrestler was somehow God himself.

By the time of Israel's prophets at the end of the Old Testament era, it was well established that God could appear on earth with a body. The third chapter of Daniel describes how three faithful Jews were thrown into a fiery furnace. When King Nebuchadnezzar peered into the flames, he exclaimed, "I see four men unbound, walking in the midst of the fire, and they are not hurt; and the appearance of the fourth is like a son of the gods" (Dan. 3:25). Nebuchadnezzar concluded that Israel's God must be the greatest, for "there is no other god who is able to rescue in this way" (v. 29). Who was this fourth man? He was a humanoid manifestation of God's saving power in the midst of the deadly fire.

Likewise, the prophet Malachi recorded God's promise: "'Behold, I send my messenger, and he will prepare the way *before me*. And the Lord whom you seek will suddenly come to his temple; and the messenger of the covenant in whom you delight, behold, he is coming,' says the Lord of hosts"

(3:1, italics mine). Let's connect this verse with another relevant Scripture. The prophet Isaiah identified the messenger's proclamation as, "In the wilderness prepare the way of the LORD; make straight in the desert a highway *for our God*" (Isa. 40:3, italics mine). Now consider what these two verses are saying when they are put side by side. The preparatory messenger was John the Baptist, according to Mark 1:2–4. He was commanded to make a straight path, not for a mere man, but for the LORD God himself. The one who came after the messenger would be God on earth!

At the close of the Old Testament era, the Jewish people were longing for God's entrance into history. He wouldn't just be a force of nature but would arrive in humanoid form. Yet this figure, who would be as great as God himself, wasn't yet considered his Son. To fully understand this idea—that the heavenly deities can have sons—we must first investigate Greek thought during the four hundred years between the end of the Old Testament and the beginning of the New. By the time of Jesus's birth, the Greek notion of a divine son had become established in Judaism as well.

Greek Sons of God

Anyone who encounters Greek mythology is struck at once by the promiscuous nature of the gods. They come down from Mount Olympus in various forms and copulate with humans, creating demigods as their offspring. The muscular and mighty Hercules is a prime example—the son of Zeus's tryst with a mortal woman. Because of his great deeds like slaying monsters and overcoming obstacles, Hercules was raised to the status of a god. Such beings were known as heroes. Greek religion had many such beings who were either children of gods or heroic humans elevated to divine rank because of their accomplishments. Although Judaism

Hercules and the Hydra by Antonio del Pollaiuolo, ca. 1475.

between the two biblical Testaments didn't accept this promiscuous understanding of God, the Greek idea of divine offspring did begin to find a home in Jewish imagination during this time.

Many educated Greeks found the crude myths of the gods distasteful. Instead, they tended to use the gods as symbols of philosophical truths. They also began to imagine that behind all the silliness of figures like Zeus, Apollo, and Aphrodite, there must be a single divinity who was higher than the rest. The foremost Greek philosopher, Plato, considered this highest god as the creator of the universe. Yet such a lofty being was so far distant from the world that he was barely knowable by anyone. In Plato's story of the world's creation, known as the *Timaeus*, he wrote, "Now to find the maker and father of this universe is hard enough, and even if I succeeded, to declare him to everyone is impossible."[1] So remote was this universal father and maker that he employed a craftsman called the Demiurge to do the actual work of construction. Even the unbelieving Plato realized that the cosmic architect needed to send out a trusted carpenter to get the job done!

The Jewish philosopher Philo was born only a few years before Jesus. He attempted to meld Greek intellectualism—particularly the thought of Plato—with the law of Moses. In one of his writings, he referred to the Word of God as the "high priest" of the world and God's "firstborn son."[2] These ideas sound an awful lot like what Christians would later recognize about Jesus of Nazareth.

Engraving of Philo of Alexandra, 1584.

Other Jewish writings composed during the intertestamental period (which means they were highly influenced by Greek thought) spoke of a soon-to-arrive "righteous man" who called himself the child of God or claimed God as his heavenly Father.[3] The famous Dead Sea Scrolls also referred to the Messiah as the Son of God.

Taken together, these Greek and Jewish ideas created a deep awareness among the people of Israel that the God who reigned in heaven needed an intermediary to carry out his will on earth. This agent couldn't be a natural force or a disembodied Word or Breath but had to be someone from within God's personal existence. He couldn't be external to God. He had to come from within the divine self. Who else could fulfill such an intimate role but a son? To the ancient way of thinking, sons were the perfect candidates for being sent out as representatives. Their main job was obedient service to the father and accurate revelation of him.

In biblical times, when royal fathers had a job to do, they would send out their princes. Once the prince arrived, it was as if the king himself were present. For example, when King

David defeated one of his enemies, a friend of David's named King Toi wanted to congratulate him since they had both fought against the same bad guy (2 Sam. 8:9–10). Instead of leaving his realm, King Toi sent his son, Joram, to ask about David's health, bless him, and convey gifts of silver and gold. When Joram was in David's presence, King Toi was essentially there as well. Sons come from fathers, they do what fathers wish, and they perfectly represent their fathers like a "chip off the old block." There can be no better representation of a father than a good son.

But what about Yahweh? We might be tempted to think that the God of monotheistic faith wouldn't have a son like this. Perhaps he should always remain solitary and alone. However, the people of Old Testament times didn't have such a limited conception of their deity. They had figured out how to uphold the Shema—"Hear, O Israel: The LORD our God, the LORD is one!"—while at the same time recognizing that so glorious a God would surely manifest his presence on earth in humanoid form. During the intertestamental era, the Jews got more comfortable with the idea of God having a servant and mediator who was so special that he could be called a divine "son." Now all they had to do was recognize the righteous son when he arrived.

As the first century AD dawned, the time was right for the birth of God's Son. The world was ready for his entrance onto the stage of history. The words of Galatians 4:4 perfectly capture what was about to happen: "But when the fullness of time had come, God sent forth his Son, born of woman, born under the law." Amazingly, a baby born from a Jewish peasant named Mary and born under the many regulations of the Jewish law would go on to become the savior of the entire world!

Part 2

Jesus: Fully God and Fully Man

5

Jesus the Son of God

Even though today's Christians consider Jesus to be the Son of God, it's worth asking whether he ever portrayed himself as such. He obviously referred to God as a heavenly Father—but was that just a generalized statement applicable to everyone? "Your Father knows what you need before you ask him," Jesus told his followers in Matthew 6:8. Then, in the next verse, he taught his disciples to pray, "Our Father in heaven, hallowed be your name" (v. 9). Clearly, God can be understood as everyone's Father, a universal paternal figure. Was Jesus his Son in the same way that we're all God's beloved children? Or was Jesus something more—a unique Son who had come down from heaven to the earthly realm? To examine Jesus's perception of himself, we must turn to the four Gospels of the New Testament as our primary source of evidence.

Gospel Depictions of God's Son

All Bible commentators have noticed a distinct difference between the first three Gospels—Matthew, Mark, and Luke—and the fourth one, the Gospel of John. The first three have a similar structure, with many stories overlapping and sometimes even using identical wording. For this reason, the first three Gospels are called the Synoptics, which means they "see together"—that is, they have the same outlook. John's Gospel stands apart in its theological perspective and its presentation of the Christ story.

The synoptic Jesus is portrayed as God's Son in a notably different way than the Johannine Jesus. In the synoptic writers, we find far less emphasis on Jesus coming down out of heaven. Instead, he is a man from here on earth who is divinely conceived and filled with heavenly power. He is a true human being with godly power to heal, preach, and exorcise demons. His ministry is enabled by God's own Spirit. Sometimes, this earth-centered depiction of Jesus is called a "Christology from below," as opposed to the Johannine "Christology from above" that we will examine in a moment.

Let us first consider the conception and birth of Jesus as depicted by two of the synoptic writers, Matthew and Luke. In Matthew 1:18, we read, "Now the birth of Jesus Christ took place in this way. When his mother Mary had been betrothed to Joseph, *before they came together* she was found to be with child from the Holy Spirit" (italics mine). The phrase "before they came together" politely refers to the absence of sexual union. Mary was a virgin when the baby Jesus was conceived in her womb. That certainly isn't normal! How did such an incredible thing happen?

Matthew doesn't tell us much. He only says this marvelous event was "from the Holy Spirit." The preposition "from" is *ek*, which means "from out of" or "by means of." All that can be determined based on Matthew's account is that the Spirit of God, rather than any human father, was the agent of the virginal conception.

Luke gives us a little more detail. He records that an angel told Mary, "The Holy Spirit will *come upon* you, and the power of the Most High will *overshadow* you; therefore the child to be born will be called holy—the Son of God" (Luke 1:35, italics mine). Notice the two key words that I have italicized: "Come upon" is *eperchomai*, which means "to descend onto something from above." The power of God was coming down upon Mary, creating a baby within her womb.

"Overshadow" is even more interesting. It is the word *episkiazo*, "to cast a shadow over something." Today, to

The Annunciation by Luca Giordano, 1672.

69

"throw shade" at someone—public ridicule or the hurling of insults—is a negative act. But in biblical times when the sun was hot and sometimes dangerous, shade was protective and good. "The Lord is your shade on your right hand," says Psalm 121:5–6, "The sun shall not strike you by day." When the Holy Spirit overshadowed Mary, he was doing something beneficial. God's presence was working something great inside her. The Greek version of the Old Testament used the same word, *episkiazo*, when it said, "And Moses was not able to enter into the tabernacle of testimony, because the cloud overshadowed it, and the tabernacle was filled with the glory of the Lord" (Exod. 40:35).[1] When God overshadows something, he causes his glory to come to that holy place.

So the synoptic stories about Jesus's birth reveal that while he was born of a woman like everyone else, he was conceived by divine agency. What about his own self-perception? Did the adult Jesus know he was God's Son?

In the Synoptic Gospels, Jesus often refers to himself as the Son of Man. Much scholarly ink has been spilled to try and define this term. It didn't just mean he was a human son (though he was truly and physically born of Mary). This phrase referred back to the book of Daniel and was a messianic term for someone who would come with great power. The prophet wrote, "Behold, with the clouds of heaven there came one like a son of man, and he came to the Ancient of Days and was presented before him. And to him was given dominion and glory and a kingdom, that all peoples, nations, and languages should serve him; his dominion is an everlasting dominion, which shall not pass away, and his kingdom one that shall not be destroyed" (Dan. 7:13–14). Clearly, when Jesus called himself the Son of Man eighty-two times in the New Testament, he meant to identify himself as the promised, glorious king from God.

In addition to this term, Jesus called himself the Son of God. Perhaps the best example was when he was directly asked if this term applied to him and he answered in the affirmative, resulting in charges of blasphemy. At Jesus's trial in Matthew 26, the high priest said to him, "I adjure you by the living God, tell us if you are the Christ, the Son of God" (v. 63). Jesus's reply was, "You have said so" (v. 64). His meaning was, "You have just stated the obvious. You've said it yourself!" He went on to add that "from now on you will see the Son of Man seated at the right hand of Power and coming on the clouds of heaven" (v. 64). Notice how for Jesus, the titles Son of God and Son of Man were equivalent. He could use them interchangeably. Both meant that he had been sent by God as his unique and chosen emissary.

But was Jesus God himself? Though the Christology from below was somewhat reluctant to come out and say this in so many words, it was clearly implied. Consider the miracle in which a paralyzed man was let down through the roof and Jesus healed him (Mark 2:1–12). Before giving the man what he wanted—legs that worked—Jesus said, "Son, your sins are forgiven" (v. 5). This got the scribes grumbling. "Why does this man speak like that? He is blaspheming! Who can forgive sins but God alone?" (v. 7).

Aware of what they were thinking, Jesus demanded to know whether it was easier to declare sins forgiven or raise up a paralyzed person. "'But that you may know that the Son of Man has authority on earth to forgive sins'—he said to the paralytic—'I say to you, rise, pick up your bed, and go home'" (vv. 10–11). When the man stood up from his mat, everyone marveled. Jesus had just declared his equality with God, not only by healing a man but by forgiving his sins.

Jesus functioned as God's Son in precisely the way that ancient sons were supposed to: by representing the father in his absence and carrying out his will. This was the point of

Jesus's parable of the wicked tenants in Matthew 21:33–44. He recounted how a landowner built a vineyard and leased it to tenants while he was absent. The landowner eventually sent servants to collect what was due, but the wicked tenants beat those servants and even killed some of them. The abused servants symbolize the Old Testament prophets who spoke God's message but were rejected in Israel.

Finally the landowner thought, "I will send my son. Surely they will respect him." In other words, the son wasn't a mere messenger. He was the representative of the master himself! Yet the wicked tenants killed even the son, earning terrible wrath from the rightful owner of the land. In the same way, Jesus represented his heavenly Father but shockingly received scorn and even violence. Jesus understood himself as God's Son who had come to do his Father's perfect will, no matter the cost. The key ideas here are sending and obedience.

When we get to John's Gospel (which was composed quite a few years after the Synoptics), we find these same ideas, yet also some new ones. The depiction of Jesus as an obedient son sent from the Father can be found in the fourth Gospel, just like the first three. Jesus declared, "I have come down from heaven, not to do my own will but the will of him who sent me" (John 6:38).

But unlike the Jesus we find in the Synoptics—a divinely conceived and empowered man—the Christology from above wasn't squeamish about depicting the descent of a heavenly being who did his Father's will. John's prologue describes how the Word was with God (1:1) and was at the Father's side in the beginning (1:18) but became flesh to dwell among us (1:14). So equal were they that Jesus could plainly state, "I and the Father are one" (10:30). The Son of Man descended from heaven (3:13) and "he who comes from above is above all" (3:31). Jesus's food was to do the work of the God who had sent him (4:34). "The Son can do nothing of his own accord, but only what he sees the Father doing. For whatever the Father does, that the Son does likewise" (5:19).

So now we have a full picture. What we can see more vaguely—though indubitably!—in the Synoptic Gospels is made clear and unequivocal in the Gospel of John. By God's overshadowing power, Jesus was conceived in the womb of a virgin. He wasn't just a holy man or wonder-worker, but God in the flesh. The heavenly Father sent his Son into the world to do what the Jewish prophets could not: provide ultimate revelation of God's saving plan and even be the instrument of that plan through his death and resurrection. In Jesus of Nazareth, the Son of God had arrived on earth!

The Apostolic Witness

If Jesus conceived of himself as God's unique Son (which is abundantly clear), did the first Christians agree with that assessment? They most certainly did, for they had proof of it beyond what Jesus said or did during his lifetime. It was the glorious resurrection of the Savior that proved his divine sonship most securely. We see this belief right from the beginning of the church, from the earliest Christian words ever recorded.

Although the letters of Paul were the first Christian documents to be written (preceding the composition of the Synoptic Gospels by

Uncial 0105, a manuscript of the Greek New Testament.

73

a few years), we occasionally get glimpses from the time before Paul put his pen to his papyrus to write a letter. Sometimes, he would quote a tradition that had been passed down to him from a previous Christian generation. He did this, for example, in his salutation to the Roman church when he explained the message he was preaching. It was the gospel that God "promised beforehand through his prophets in the holy Scriptures, concerning his Son, who was descended from David according to the flesh and was declared to be the Son of God in power according to the Spirit of holiness by his resurrection from the dead, Jesus Christ our Lord" (Rom. 1:2–4). These weren't Paul's own words but a creedal formula that he already knew. He quoted it to assure the Romans that he held the same gospel they had embraced.

We also know that the very earliest Christians applied one of the Old Testament psalms to Jesus as proof of his divine sonship. The psalm says, "You are my son; today I

Ceiling mosaic in the Baptistery of Neon depicting the baptism of Jesus. Photo by Petar Milošević (Wikimedia Commons, CC BY 4.0).

have become your father" (Ps. 2:7 NIV). In all three synoptic accounts of Jesus's baptism, a similar pronouncement is made by a heavenly voice when Jesus comes up out of the water: "You are my beloved Son; with you I am well pleased" (Matt. 3:17; Mark 1:11; Luke 3:22). Many reliable Greek manuscripts of the Synoptic Gospels quote God's statement this way, which is why it is printed in modern Bible versions. Yet some ancient manuscripts instead quoted Psalm 2:7 at this point, with its comment, "Today I have become your father" (NIV). Obviously, some early copyists thought this was what God had said when Jesus emerged from the water, though the words printed in contemporary Bible versions are more likely to be accurate.

But aside from what may or may not have been said at Jesus's baptism, Psalm 2 is directly applied to him three times elsewhere in the New Testament. The apostle Paul used the verse to prove to the synagogue rulers that Jesus's resurrection displayed him to be the Son of God (Acts 13:33). The writer to the Hebrews argued from Psalm 2 that the Son of God is vastly more glorious than angels (1:5) and is an eternal high priest (5:5). These early Christian pronouncements confirm the widespread belief that Jesus was the long-awaited Son of God.

Numerous other instances from the letters of Paul could be put on the table to support the early belief that Jesus was God's Son. We have already mentioned Galatians 4:4: "When the fullness of time had come, God sent forth his Son, born of woman, born under the law." Or consider 1 Thessalonians 1:10, which says that we "wait for his Son from heaven, whom he raised from the dead, Jesus who delivers us from the wrath to come." Paul's gospel proclaimed the crucified and risen Son of God.

The apostle Peter wholeheartedly agreed with his coworker and comrade. Perhaps he believed it even more strongly than

Paul. Why? Because he had stood on the mountain of transfiguration and remembered how God's thunderous voice had reaffirmed the baptismal pronouncement, "This is my beloved Son, with whom I am well pleased" (Matt. 17:5; Mark 9:7; Luke 9:35; 2 Pet. 1:17). Peter had no doubts about Jesus's sonship. We know this because he exclaimed in one of his letters, "Blessed be the God and Father of our Lord Jesus Christ!" (1 Pet. 1:3).

Likewise, the book of Revelation proclaims Jesus as a divine Son. Using the same language as Daniel, Jesus in heaven is described as a glorious "son of man" (Rev. 1:13; 14:14). He has "freed us from our sins by his blood and made us a kingdom, priests to his God and Father" (1:5–6). The letter to the church at Thyatira calls its author "the Son of God, who has eyes like a flame of fire, and whose feet are like burnished bronze" (2:18). The faithful Christians of Sardis will rejoice when Jesus confesses their names before his Father (3:5), and the Laodicean believers are promised they will sit on Jesus's throne just as he sat down on his Father's (3:21). The glorious Lamb of God can be seen standing on Mount Zion with 144,000 followers "who had his name and his Father's name written on their foreheads" (14:1).

For the early church, then, there could be no question that Jesus was the Son of God. The witness of the New Testament was unanimous from the first Gospels to the book of Revelation. Yet one obvious question remained. How was the glory of God's Son related to the glory of his Father? Was their glory equal in every way, or was the Son's slightly lesser? After all, sons derive their source from their fathers and are sent as obedient representatives. Doesn't this mean that sons—even highly honored firstborn sons—are "secondary" to the one who generated them and sent them out? If so, should Christians think that way about God's Son?

Was he lesser than his heavenly Father in any way? Or were they essentially equal from all time?

This was the great Trinitarian question that would vex the Christian church for its first three hundred years until clarity was achieved at the Council of Nicaea. And even afterward, as we will soon see, the matter continued to be debated. The story of the Trinity had many twists and turns before the Nicene Creed finally gained universal acceptance as an accurate explanation of God's truth.

6

Maybe Jesus *Is* the Father?

After Jesus went back to heaven, he sent out his followers as eyewitnesses of his teachings and deeds. His messengers included more than his inner circle of twelve apostles. The risen Christ appeared to at least five hundred of his disciples, some of whom went on to live for decades afterward (1 Cor. 15:6). They scattered across the world to testify about their experience with the Savior. This first generation of believers could proclaim "that which was from the beginning, which we have heard, which we have seen with our eyes, which we looked upon and have touched with our hands, concerning the word of life" (1 John 1:1). They had walked with Jesus during his earthly life or witnessed him after he rose from the dead. They could speak from their firsthand experiences. But what would happen after this original generation of eyewitnesses passed off the scene when the first century came to a close?

The Christians from the second to the fifth century are collectively known as the "early church fathers." Of course, this doesn't mean there were no church mothers! But since women rarely wrote books in those days, we have many more writings from men, so we use the term "fathers" as a catch-all expression. As we begin to encounter their theological views on the way to the Council of Nicaea, let's pause to consider a framework for understanding these early centuries of church history. Many believers today don't know much about this era, so it's worth taking a moment to sketch out a basic timeline.

The idea of the "first century AD" is easily under-standable. We use BC to describe the years "before Christ" and AD for the years from his birth onward. AD stands for *anno Domini*, which is Latin for "in the year of the Lord."

Timeline of the First Four Centuries

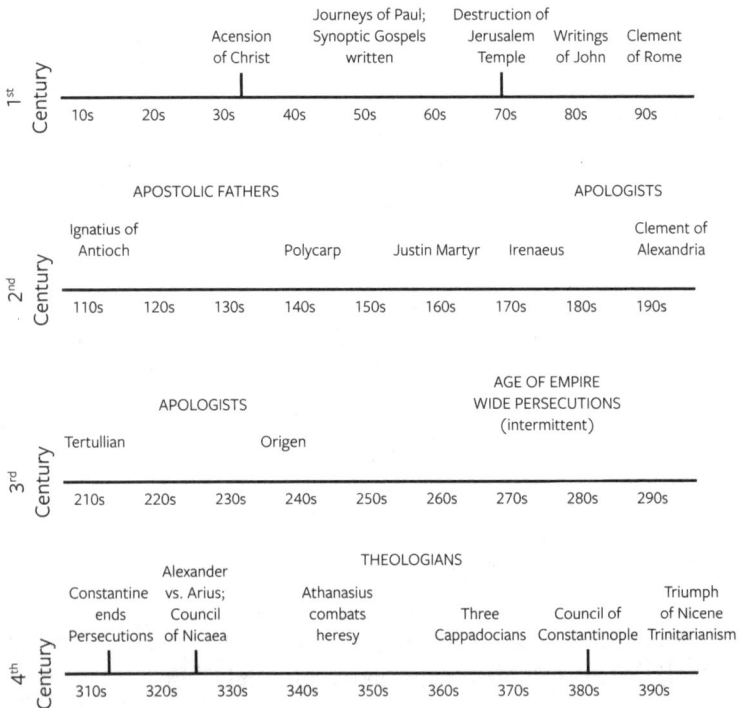

1st Century

		Ascension of Christ		Journeys of Paul; Synoptic Gospels written		Destruction of Jerusalem Temple	Writings of John	Clement of Rome
10s	20s	30s	40s	50s	60s	70s	80s	90s

2nd Century

APOSTOLIC FATHERS   APOLOGISTS

Ignatius of Antioch			Polycarp		Justin Martyr	Irenaeus		Clement of Alexandria
110s	120s	130s	140s	150s	160s	170s	180s	190s

3rd Century

APOLOGISTS   AGE OF EMPIRE WIDE PERSECUTIONS (intermittent)

Tertullian		Origen						
210s	220s	230s	240s	250s	260s	270s	280s	290s

4th Century

THEOLOGIANS

Constantine ends Persecutions	Alexander vs. Arius; Council of Nicaea	Athanasius combats heresy			Three Cappadocians	Council of Constantinople	Triumph of Nicene Trinitarianism
310s	320s	330s	340s	350s	360s	370s	380s	390s

Jesus lived on earth until about AD 33. Paul's missionary journeys and letters date to the 40s to 60s, and both he and Peter were martyred in the late 60s. The Synoptic Gospels were probably written before 70, when the Romans destroyed the Jewish temple in Jerusalem. The apostle John lived into the 90s, so his letters, Gospel, and Apocalypse (the book of Revelation) were all written or finalized between 70 and the mid-90s. The first century ended in the year 99.

The second century encompasses the years 100–199. During its early decades, the Christian leaders could remember the apostles or had been in touch with the original generation, so we call them the "apostolic fathers." They would include Clement of Rome, Ignatius of Antioch, and Papias. Their writings tended to be pastoral instead of theological. Christians were few in number at this time, led faithfully by their obscure pastors.

But later in the second century and on into the third, the Roman Empire became more aware of Christianity. This led to a lot of criticism and sometimes even persecution. We call the figures of this era the "apologists" because their more sophisticated writings attempted to make an apologetic defense of the true faith against pagan hostility. Some famous names include Justin Martyr, Irenaeus, Clement of Alexandria, Tertullian, and Origen.

Engraving of Tertullian, 1584. Image by The Trustees of the British Museum (Wikimedia Commons, CC BY-NC-SA 4.0).

Things changed dramatically for the church at the beginning of the fourth century. In 313, Emperor Constantine decided not only to end Roman persecution but to convert to the Christian faith himself. Though he was a man on a spiritual journey who only gradually left behind his pagan ways, he certainly did help Christianity find a more solid cultural footing. As we will see in an upcoming chapter, it was Constantine who convened the Council of Nicaea in 325. The Trinitarian debate would rage on for the next few decades, giving the name "theologians" to the church fathers of that era. This big doctrinal controversy was more or less resolved by 399, the end of the fourth century. Forever afterward, all Christians—whether Roman Catholics, Eastern Orthodox, or Protestants—believed basically the same things about the Trinity. Anybody who denied this doctrine would be viewed as standing outside the historic Christian faith. Though some people (mostly among the Germanic tribes) did deny the Trinity, they eventually came around to the same view as everyone else.

Before we can get to that end point, however, we need to examine the important steps along the way. After Jesus ascended to heaven and his eyewitnesses passed off the scene, the church fathers of the second and third centuries began to try and make sense of the biblical data that we have already examined. The Bible says Jesus is the Son of God? Check! And Jesus is divine? Check! But was Jesus "God" in exactly the same way that God the Father was "God"? Or was Jesus's deity, though still great and glorious, a little bit lesser than his Father's?

Or perhaps we could say—now here's an interesting idea!—that Jesus was actually God the Father himself? Maybe God the Father morphed into God the Son and came down to earth. Would this be the best way of preserving Jewish monotheism while still affirming the full deity of Christ?

As it turned out, this concept had fundamental flaws that made it unviable. Nevertheless, the church fathers needed to grapple with it on the way to finding the right view. Let's take a look at this idea that represented a stumbling block on the road to Nicaea.

Ancient Church Modalism

Adolf von Harnack, the great twentieth-century historian at the University of Berlin, coined the term "modalism" to describe the ancient church thesis that God the Father was the same person as God the Son. The idea here was that God presented himself in successive "modes" or ways of revealing himself to humans. In the act of creation, God was known as a Father. In the act of redemption, he was then known as a Son. In the act of inspiring and indwelling the church, he was finally known as a Spirit. Yet in each case, he was the exact same being. We humans were just seeing different aspects of him, all lined up in a sequence.

At first glance, this doesn't sound so bad. In fact, many of our modern analogies of the Trinity are types of modalism. Well-meaning Christians use these illustrations to try and explain the Three-in-One. One of the most common examples is the H_2O illustration. "Look at an ice cube," we might say. "It is cold and hard, but when it melts, it is seen in a new mode. When we boil it to steam, there is a third mode. The same molecules can be experienced as a solid, liquid, or vapor. The Trinity is like that too." Another common example is the analogy of an egg. We experience a shell, a white, and a yolk; yet it is one egg. Similarly, a single apple has its skin, its flesh, and its core. All of these are ways of encountering a single object through three distinct experiences.

Here's another illustration. Consider the child's puzzle called the Pyraminx. This toy from the 1980s, like the

Rubik's Cube, had movable facets designed to be arranged into sides of the same color. But unlike a six-sided cube, the Pyraminx had only three sides that formed a pyramid shape (actually four sides, but for the sake of illustration, let's exclude the bottom). If a solved Pyraminx were sitting on a table, one side would be

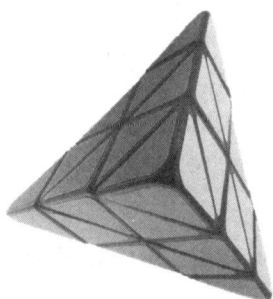

Pyraminx by Colin Hall (Wikimedia Commons, CC BY-SA-3.0).

orange, another side green, and a third side yellow. You could turn this toy around and experience three distinct facets—yet it is one single object. Is this like the Trinity?

The ancient modalists thought so, though they didn't use Harnack's term to describe themselves. They were originally known as Monarchians, meaning they held to the "sole rule" (*monarchia*) of God. Their ideas were especially well-received at Rome, often among the simple, uneducated Christians, yet even by some of the more learned bishops who should have known better. Around 200, a man from Smyrna named Noetus began to spread these ideas. His disciple Epigonus showed up in Rome and gained a wide following. Another Monarchian teacher was Praxeas. His name means "busybody," so perhaps this was a derogatory nickname for one of Rome's bishops, Pope Callistus. There is evidence that Callistus leaned toward Monarchianism.

The foremost Monarchian was Sabellius, a more intellectual thinker than the others. Later generations of Christians who didn't like this view of God referred to it as the heresy of Sabellianism. Some critics also called it Patripassianism, which meant that God the Father suffered the passion of the cross. Think about that for a moment. Does it give you concern? Are Christians supposed to say that God the Father was nailed hand and foot to the tree of Calvary? Didn't the Father remain in heaven while sending his Son for that task? Yes, he did. The Father and Son must be separate enough to have had distinct experiences. Something just didn't sound right about modalism or Patripassianism, as the ancient Christians who opposed it were quick to point out.

Yet the modalists believed they had a few Bible verses on their side. Some of their most quoted evidence (using the New Living Translation to make things clear) included:

- Isaiah 45:14: "God is with you, and he is the only God. There is no other."
- John 10:30: "The Father and I are one."
- John 14:9: "Jesus replied, 'Have I been with you all this time, Philip, and yet you still don't know who I am? Anyone who has seen me has seen the Father!'"
- Romans 9:5: "Christ himself was an Israelite as far as his human nature is concerned. And he is God, the one who rules over everything and is worthy of eternal praise!"

You can see that these verses do equate God and Jesus. Some kind of equivalence must exist between them. "Just follow the Scriptures!" cried the modalists. "These two are the same being. They are one. There's no one else!" That might sound like a good idea. But as we have already said, the full biblical picture made room for distinctness between the Father and Son along with their equality. There had to be a better way than modalism to express the divine relationship. No one knew this better than Tertullian of Carthage, the sharp-minded (and sharp-tongued) African church father. He was the first person in church history to use the term

"Trinity" to describe the Three-in-One. And he gave us two more terms of great theological importance: "person" and "substance." Let's examine them now.

Tertullian Against Praxeas

The modalist called Praxeas began spreading his pseudo-Trinitarian ideas far and wide. When his view crossed from the boot of Italy into North Africa—to today's nation of Tunisia where ancient Carthage was located—the city's foremost Christian thinker drew his six-shooter and began to fire theological bullets at this unbiblical doctrine. The very first line of Tertullian's treatise *Against Praxeas*, written in 213, claims that his opponent was voicing the devil's own views. Of course, the modalists weren't actually so diabolical. Their theology was a well-meaning but erroneous attempt to preserve the idea of one God. They desperately wanted to avoid slipping back into the multiple gods of pagan polytheism.

So what made Tertullian and other anti-modalists so upset? They objected to how the individuality of Christ's personhood was violated when he was turned into a mere mode of the divine substance. According to the whole witness of Scripture, God the Father was one person while Jesus his Son was another. They interacted with each other in a relational way. Scripture was just too clear about this to let a few misinterpreted verses overturn such an obvious aspect of Jesus's behavior in the Gospels. The church insisted on retaining the distinct personhood of its Savior. (At this point, the nature of the Holy Spirit wasn't yet being discussed. Although that would be defined later, proper Christology had to be nailed down first.)

Tertullian criticized Praxeas for his reliance on "allegories and parables" instead of the "clearly defined and simple

86

statements" of the Bible.[1] The truth must be established by appeal not only to the "old scriptures" but also the New Testament.[2] When a few difficult-to-understand passages appear, they mustn't drive the cart of exegesis but must yield to the total proclamation of God's Word. For example, Jesus's remark to Philip that "whoever has seen me has seen the Father" (John 14:9), which was popular among the modalists because it seemed to equate the Father and Son, can't contradict the whole witness of the fourth Gospel that the Son is someone other than the Father. Tertullian goes on for page after page showing that John's Christology from above depicts the Savior who came down from heaven as someone distinct from the God who sent him.

One of Tertullian's evidences against Praxeas was Jesus's anguished cry from the cross, "My God, my God, why have you forsaken me?" (Matt. 27:46). To whom did Jesus address this cry—himself? That makes no sense. Jesus was crying out to his Father in heaven at that climactic moment in salvation history. Tertullian backed up his interpretation by correlating this verse with the God who "did not spare his own Son but gave him up for us all" (Rom. 8:32) and who "laid on him the iniquity of us all" (Isa. 53:6). Clearly, God the Father was the sender and offerer of his Son, while Jesus was the sent one and the sacrifice who was offered. They weren't the same being like the modalists claimed. They were distinct from one another.

But if they were distinct, what exactly were they? What term should be used to display their separateness? Each of them was a distinct . . . what?

Tertullian answered this question with an important word in Christian theology: "person." His formula, which he introduced in *Against Praxeas*, would prove very influential on the proper Christian way to think about the Trinity. He reserved the word "person" for the three individual existences of the Trinity. They weren't just modes of self-revelation, each experienced sequentially, like ice becoming water then steam. The Bible never depicts Jesus as God the Father in disguise. For example, in the garden of Gethsemane, Jesus wasn't praying to himself when he asked his Father to "take this cup from me" (Luke 22:42 NIV). Nonsense! A true person was praying to another person in that moment.

Yet these distinct persons were united in their deity. To define how this worked, Tertullian turned to the word "substance." This term, like "person," would prove to be a landmark of Christian theological thinking in the years to come. Tertullian declared, "I always maintain one substance in three who cohere" (*unam substantiam in tribus cohaerentibus*).[3] For all of Tertullian's faults—and they were many in this fiery defender of the faith—he bequeathed to the ancient church the vital idea of a *Trinitas* that consisted of one divine "substance" and three distinct "persons." Amazingly, this would be exactly what the Council of Nicaea would endorse more than a hundred years later.

So, was Tertullian a great hero who solved the Trinitarian problem once and for all? Did the famous council just put a rubber stamp on his earlier ideas? Hardly! Though Tertullian was a creative thinker who advanced the ball far down the field, he fumbled the pigskin before scoring a touchdown. How so?

Tertullian held that the Word of God, or Logos—the Second Person of the Trinity—had existed for all eternity with the Father and the Holy Spirit. That's sound doctrine. John 1:1 says about Jesus, "In the beginning was the Word [*logos*]." However, Tertullian went astray when he said the Logos wasn't a Son during that whole time and only *became* a Son when God sent him forth on mission. In other words, the Second Person was eternal—but only as the Logos. His sonship, Tertullian believed, had a moment of beginning.

This erroneous view might not seem like a big deal. At least Tertullian wasn't denying the eternity of the Second Person! Yet the ancient church wasn't ready to accept a God who wasn't always a Father to his beloved Son. Fatherhood and sonship had to be inherent within the eternal Trinity. In the next chapter, we will discover how a defense of this crucial idea came from Origen of Alexandria, the brilliant Egyptian theologian. It was yet another important development on the road to Nicaea.

7

Always a Father, Always a Son

It is an interesting but little-known historical fact that the Christian doctrine of the Trinity in its proper, orthodox form was pioneered mostly by Africans. We have already met the African church father Tertullian, a native of Carthage in modern Tunisia, who contributed so much to the vocabulary and preliminary conceptualization of the *Trinitas*. Yet Tertullian failed to recognize that paternity and filiation—fancy words for fatherhood and sonship—were essential to the eternal Godhead. There never was a time when God the Father did not have God the Son as his offspring.

But wait—that's a very strange idea! In our everyday experience, fathers do not always have sons. The very idea of a biological father means that he's *not* one until he impregnates a woman. Then and only then does a man become a "father." Most Christians understand there isn't a divine Mother within the Trinity, so that isn't a theological conundrum for us at this time. But what about the chronological element? What about the fact that there is always a time when men are nonfathers, and then they become fathers once they have a kid? Maybe

Tertullian was correct to say that the eternal God *became* a Father when his Logos became his Son. At least then it would fit with our human experience that children aren't eternal but are sourced within their parents and find their beginnings from them. Could Tertullian have gotten this right?

And while we're on the topic of sons, let's figure out the proper word for their origins or beginnings. When it comes to the father's side of the bargain, there isn't a great English term to use. Mothers have the common term "conception" to describe what happens to them when they conceive a child in their wombs. What about a masculine term? A man might be said to "father" his offspring, using his descriptive word as a verb instead of a noun. But that's a little repetitive: "A father fathers his son." And we can't really apply the verb "sire" to humans as if they are dogs or horses with pedigreed bloodlines. That leaves us with our best available term: the old-fashioned yet still usable verb "to beget." Perhaps the King James Version of John 3:16 is familiar to you: "For God so loved the world, that he gave his only *begotten* Son, that whosoever believeth in him should not perish, but have everlasting life" (italics mine). For the purposes of this chapter, let's adopt the terminology of "begotten" and "begetting" as our primary fathering words. We can also speak of a father's "generation" of his son as basically the same thing. We will try to explore the Trinitarian implications of these terms in Scripture and among the church fathers.

Engraving of Origen by Guillaume Chaudière, 1584.

As we begin to confront Tertullian's idea that begetting wasn't eternal with God but started at a specific point in time, we'll need to engage with another African architect of Trinitarian thought. He was the great scholar Origen of Alexandria, an Egyptian who possessed one of the most brilliant minds that the Christian church has ever known. Such brilliance can be both a blessing and a curse, for while it enables great ideas to be imagined, it also magnifies errors when deep thoughts go down the wrong track.

Such was the case with Origen. He was like the character in one of Henry Wadsworth Longfellow's poems:

> There was a little girl,
>   And she had a little curl
> Right in the middle of her forehead.
>   When she was good
>   She was very, very good,
> And when she was bad she was horrid.[1]

In this book, we won't dwell upon the theological areas where Origen was "horrid." Instead, we'll remember how "very, very good" he was at finding a way for Christians to speak about God's eternal Trinitarian relationship of paternity and filiation. God the Father has always had God the Son at his side. How do we describe this?

Economic Trinitarianism

The earliest thinkers about the Trinity, like Tertullian or his forerunner, Irenaeus of Lyons, gave much theological attention to the way that God acts in the world. Although he is enthroned on high, he can still project his formative power into his creation. Aspects of himself go forth to accomplish tasks. This is essentially the old Hebraic idea that the one God acts on earth though his Word and his Breath. The Second and Third Persons of the Trinity do whatever the First Person (i.e., God the Father) commands. Irenaeus said that when the three persons decided, "Let us make man in our image, after our likeness" (Gen. 1:26), the original man, Adam, was molded from the soil by the Father's two "hands": the Son and the Spirit.[2] Tertullian agreed with Irenaeus that the Second and Third Persons exist to carry out the orders of the First Person. As Jesus himself declared, "I seek not my own will but the will of him who sent me" (John 5:30).

As Irenaeus and Tertullian considered the Trinity's mutual intention to accomplish great things in the cosmos—not just its creation, but eventually its salvation—they used the key term *oikonomia*. Even though Tertullian wrote in Latin, he quoted this Greek word in addition to its Latin equivalent, which was *dispensatio* or *dispositio*. The modern word that we derive from *oikonomia* is "economy," which usually connotes money, banking, and finance. But its root meaning came from *oikos*, "house," and *nomos*, "law." An "economy" was the law of the household—that is, the way its affairs were managed. Later, it came to mean how finances were managed, but originally it meant any kind of plan put in place by the master of the house. Using Latin-based words, we could say it described how things in a household were "dispensed" or "disposed." And just like a human estate must follow the laws of its master, so God's Trinitarian household had its divinely decreed organization.

Modern historians use the term "economic Trinitarianism" to describe the ancient theological focus on how the three persons accomplish creation and redemption. The story would go something like this. In the eternal past, before God decided to make a universe, the three persons existed in perfect harmony. They always interacted with one another in complete relational fulfillment. During this time, the idea of God's Word (or sometimes, his Wisdom) was sufficient to describe the Second Person. He was an intimate conversation partner with the other two persons. Not yet was there any need to send him out. His existence consisted only of a loving relationship with the other members of the Trinity. That was the "law of the household" at first.

But then the First Person declared his intention to make a universe. Now God needed someone "sendable" to carry out his commands. In other words, he needed a Son; for as we have already seen, sons go forth and represent their fathers. This is why Tertullian thought that the Second Person's sonship had a point of beginning. A son simply wasn't needed within the Trinity before God decided to create a cosmos (or later, to save it from sin). Once creation and salvation became part of God's expressed will, the "economic Trinity" was rearranged to carry out the plan of the Master. This would happen via God's two extensions, his metaphorical hands by which his will is accomplished. Now that obedient service was required, the eternal Word became a Son. He did this so he could be the divine instrument of creation and salvation. The Spirit cooperated in this task as well.

Although this type of thinking didn't win the day, Tertullian did have a few Bible verses that seemed to support his view. One of the primary ones was Proverbs 8, where the Wisdom of God is personified as a separate being. Since the New Testament referred to Christ as Wisdom (1 Cor. 1:24, 30), the ancient church fathers always applied the passage from Proverbs to Jesus Christ. It declared:

> The LORD formed me from the beginning, before he created anything else.
> I was appointed in ages past, at the very first, before the earth began.

I was born before the oceans were created, before the
springs bubbled forth their waters.

Before the mountains were formed, before the hills, I
was born—

before he had made the earth and fields and the first
handfuls of soil.

I was there when he established the heavens, when he
drew the horizon on the oceans. . . .

I was the architect at his side.

I was his constant delight, rejoicing always in his
presence.

And how happy I was with the world he created;

how I rejoiced with the human family! (Prov. 8:22–27,
30–31 NLT)

Clearly, this personified Wisdom was separate from the
LORD and existed prior to the creation of the cosmos as a
kind of heavenly helper.[3] Proverbs 8 seems to teach that out
of God's Wisdom, a new being was "formed" or "born" to
carry out a divine plan of creation and salvation. Tertullian thought this was when the eternal Word or Wisdom
became God's Son and made him a Father. Although this
idea appeared to have merit, it was soon to receive a sharp
challenge from one of Tertullian's fellow Africans: Origen
of Alexandria, the famous theologian and exegete.

Origen and Eternal Generation

If Tertullian had departed from the harbor of his native
Carthage and sailed eastward along the northern coast of
Africa, he eventually would have reached the metropolis of
Alexandria in the Nile River delta. There he might have met
the slightly younger Christian scholar named Origen (though

we have no reason to think a meeting between these two great thinkers ever took place). In making this hypothetical journey to Egypt, Tertullian would have entered a whole new world. The common language would have shifted from Latin to Greek. So, too, would the nature of philosophy, including Christian philosophy. Latin North Africa, being very close to Italy, was influenced by Roman law and practical concerns. But the city of Alexandria was more like today's Oxford or Cambridge, or like the campus of Harvard or Yale. In ancient times, Alexandria was the center of advanced thinking, especially the long-revered philosophy of Plato. These were the deep intellectual waters in which Origen swam. He couldn't help but be affected by them. In fact, he often gulped them down.

Origen pursued every possible line of theological inquiry. For example, he sought to understand why verses like John 3:16 referred to Jesus as God's "only begotten Son" (NKJV).[4] The Greek word here was *monogenes*. *Mono* obviously meant one, but *genes* (pronounced gen-ACE with a hard g) was more debatable. It could be from *genos*, a type or kind of something. Many modern English translators after the King James Version interpret it this way. They believe *monogenes* meant "one of a kind," so John 3:16 is often translated as "one and only Son."

But ancient Bible readers thought *genes* was instead related to the verb *gennao*, "to beget a son." Thus it would mean "only begotten," just like the King James Version translators assumed as well. This understanding, though incorrect according to some modern grammarians, was important theologically. Jesus wasn't just one of a kind; he was truly a Son "begotten" by his Father. Despite its controversial linguistic root, "only begotten" became a key idea in the Nicene Creed. And who are we to tell the ancients how to use their own words?

But even if John 3:16 involved a little controversy, the Bible was clear enough elsewhere about the Son's begetting. The Greek version of Psalm 2:7 had declared "Thou art my son, today I have begotten thee."[5] The verb used there was *gennao*. Since this verse was applied to Jesus in Acts 13:33 and Hebrews 1:5 and 5:5 (using *gennao* each time), we have clear biblical evidence that Jesus was "begotten" from the Father.

So here was a problem for Origen. The Scriptures, which he loved and respected and which he spent countless hours interpreting, said God begat a Son. Normally, that would imply a moment of beginning, as when every human father's sperm meets the egg and initiates a new life. The child starts to exist right then, and not before.

But Origen's Platonic intellectual outlook, which he also believed was valuable, told him that divine beings don't have sources or origins. A true God doesn't *begin*; he just *is*. Creatures certainly have origins, but Origen didn't want to attribute creaturely status to the Second Person of the Trinity (or Triad, which was his equivalent term in Greek). Origen believed the Second Person was fully divine, which meant he must be eternal and unchangeable. So how could the Son truly be a Son without having a temporal moment of begetting? Or if he had a beginning, how could he be God?

Origen solved the problem by proposing the doctrine of the Son's "eternal generation": that he was begotten by God the Father without any reference to time. Like a fountain eternally bubbling up from its wellspring, the Son of God always does have, and always has had, and always will have, his source within the Father. Immediately, of course, this requires clarification. Such begetting doesn't fit with the human act of sexual intercourse that results in a conception. That act always has a time element of before and after. But Origen insisted "it is impious and shocking to regard God the Father in the begetting of his only-begotten Son . . . as being similar to any human being or other animal in the act of begetting." Instead, there must be "some exceptional process, worthy of God, to which we can find no comparison whatsoever." And what was it? Origen declared, "This is an eternal and everlasting begetting, as brightness is begotten from light."[6]

Why is light a good metaphor? Because a source of light and the brightness it emits cannot be separated temporally. Light, whenever it exists, causes brightness. The brightness is always sourced in the light. Never does one exist without the other. When an oil lamp is lit (or a light bulb is switched on), the room is immediately illuminated. If a source of light were eternal, the brightness emitted from it would be eternal as well. This perfectly describes God. Origen quoted Hebrews 1:3, which declares that Christ is "the radiance of the glory of God and the exact imprint of his nature." The Son is the eternal brightness of the Father's eternal light. The two go together—always. Yet one is the cause of the other.

In this way, Origen refuted the erroneous aspect in the theology of his fellow African, Tertullian. There was never a time when the First Person wasn't a Father and the Second Person wasn't a Son. Although we can't use human begetting as a direct analogy (for that will always involve a chronological element), we can still call it a unique kind of divine begetting. Origen's concept firmly established eternal paternity and filiation within the Trinity.

Ranks Within the Godhead?

Unfortunately, as we noted above with the Longfellow poem, Origen could sometimes be "horrid." One of his theological mistakes was to differentiate the Father and Son so much that he ranked their divinity, putting one above the other. There is a sense in which that is proper, for do we not speak of the First and Second Persons? Yes, that is an acceptable way to think. But Origen tended to go further. He allowed the category of "divine" to have gradations within it. Thus, he called the Son "secondary God" and could sometimes imply that the Son was inferior, not only in his role of obedience, but even in his own essential being.

To reach a conclusion like that, Origen misinterpreted John 17:3. He took its words, "And this is eternal life, that they know you, the only true God, and Jesus Christ whom you have sent," to suggest that only God the Father was "true God." At root, this interpretation wasn't intended to demote Christ. It merely reflected Origen's desire not to be a modalist—in other words, not to equate the Father and Son as the same person. Somehow, they had to be distinct from one another. But differentiating them by making one inferior to the other wasn't the right way to address the issue.

Even more horrid was Origen's belief that the Holy Spirit was so far in the third rank that he was actually a creation of the Father and Son. That is definitely wrong! Origen's tendency to place the three persons in a graded hierarchy—with the implication that their ranks reflect varying degrees of deity—is called subordinationism. He wasn't the only church father to think that way, just the one who stated it more clearly than anyone had before.

Yet someone was about to emerge on the Christian theo-logical scene to take this idea even further. He, too, would arise from the brainy Alexandrian milieu. This figure would dare to say that the Son's inferiority was so pronounced that he wasn't even eternal. The Son, like the Spirit, was just a creature whom God had made. This man's name was Arius. Today he is considered an arch-heretic of the church. He is widely scorned for his blasphemous views. Even so, it was Arius's ideas that forced the ancient church to finally con-front the Trinitarian puzzle head on and convene the Council of Nicaea to seek a resolution.

8

The Rise of Heresy

In a church history course that I used to teach, I would sometimes play a joke on my students for the sake of illustration. I would select a student before class to help me—usually someone from the front row who had shown a willingness to ask sharp questions of the teacher. The other students would consider them a bit edgy. I gave them secret instructions on exactly what to do. Then I would begin class as normal.

During the course of my lecture on the Council of Nicaea, the chosen student would be waiting for me to declare, "Bishop Alexander believed that God and Christ were both eternal!" The moment I uttered those words, the student would initiate their prearranged role. Leaping from their seat, they would point a finger at me and cry, "Heresy! You're completely wrong! You're a false prophet! I'm sick of your blasphemy!" Then they would storm out of the room by a side door. Needless to say, the atmosphere in the lecture hall would be turned to horrified discomfort and stunned silence. An awkward shock would grip my wide-eyed students.

Playing my role, I would stare incredulously at my accomplice as they exited the room, my mouth agape.

But then I would turn back to the distressed students with a twinkle in my eye. A smile would creep to my face—not a fake one, for as a teacher, I appreciated the power of an illustration to make an idea stick. Facing everyone and gesturing to the door, I would proclaim, "That, my friends, was what happened in the year 318 when the heretic Arius challenged his bishop over theology! Give a round of applause to our actor!" The students' collective sigh of relief could be heard even among their laughter and clapping as my accomplice reentered the classroom, grinning at their mischief as they resumed their front-row seat.

Did the historical events really unfold like that? Did Arius storm out of the room after shouting at Bishop Alexander? I had to admit to my students that perhaps my skit was an exaggeration. But maybe it was close to the truth. We do know that some kind of public confrontation occurred between Arius and Alexander around 318. And we know the precise issues about which they were arguing. Those issues were so important that they prompted the Roman emperor to call a huge meeting to resolve them only seven years later. What was going on?

"There Was When He Was Not"

Arius was a Christian pastor from the country of Libya who had taken up residence in the nearby Egyptian capital of Alexandria. This thriving city, home to Origen only a few decades before, had become Arius's home as well. He lived there for many years and was an old man when the controversy broke out.

By all accounts, Arius was widely respected for his logical mind and devotion to the Scriptures. For a time, he had

Portrait of Arius. Detail of *First Council of Nicaea* by Michael Damaskinos, 1591.

served as a deacon, but by 318 he had been ordained as a preaching pastor (or "presbyter"). This meant he had his own congregation in the long-standing Christian neighborhood of Baucalis, one of nine parishes in the city. Some ancient traditions suggest that the Gospel writer Mark had been martyred in that area several centuries earlier. A famous church nearby claimed to house the apostolic grave. Although the Markan connection to Alexandria can't be firmly proven, it's not impossible.

In any case, pastoring a church in the Baucalis neighborhood—which translates to something like the "cowboy area"—meant that many of Arius's followers would have been rough (and sometimes violent) cattle herders from just outside the city walls. On the other hand, seven hundred virgin nuns in Baucalis, drawn to the nearby shrine of Saint Mark, had also devoted themselves to their local pastor's teaching. Arius found himself well-liked by people of all kinds. He had a powerful mind, a clear message, and a gift for public relations.

While Arius's theological break with Bishop Alexander might not have been as dramatic as my classroom illustration made it seem, the famous event did initiate a widening

The Corniche of Alexandria. Photo by Vyacheslav Argenberg (Wikimedia Commons, CC BY 4.0).

rupture within the Egyptian church that eventually led to the Council of Nicaea. Here is the original account of what happened from one ancient church historian:

> In the fearless exercise of his functions for the instruction and government of the church, Bishop Alexander attempted one day in the presence of the presbytery and the rest of his clergy to explain, with perhaps too much philosophical detail, that great theological mystery—the unity of the holy Trinity. A certain one of the presbyters under his jurisdiction whose name was Arius, possessing not inconsiderable logical ability, imagined that the bishop was subtly teaching the same view as Sabellius the Libyan. From a love of controversy, he took the opposite opinion to that of the Libyan and supposed that he should vigorously respond to what was said by the bishop.[1]

Notice Arius's primary concern here. He feared that his bishop, who emphasized the unity of the Trinity, might be teaching Sabellianism. We have already identified this doctrine (today called "modalism") as the incorrect view that the Father, Son, and Holy Spirit are the exact same being, just seen in different expressions or modes at different times. In other words, in modalism, the three persons aren't differentiated enough from one another. They are just different aspects of the same singular deity.

Arius wanted to go drastically in the opposite direction. He wanted to differentiate the three persons so much—even beyond the graded divinity suggested by Origen—that they couldn't be considered equal at all. Only the Father could be called eternal and uncreated. The Son and Spirit were creatures made by him and thus not "true God." This would, Arius supposed, preserve the biblical, monotheistic view of one and only one God. Of course, Bishop Alexander wanted the same thing. The question was how to express it properly. Could the Son be demoted from divine to creaturely status in order to preserve the uniqueness of the Father? Arius said yes, but this horrified his bishop, who believed the people of God were being led into false doctrine.

Like many other Christian thinkers, Arius recognized that one of the most important words in Scripture was "begotten." As we have already seen, this word means "to father a child." It's a common biblical expression. Of course, when Abraham begat Isaac, or when Isaac begat Jacob, a chronological element was involved. There was a time when the sons Isaac or Jacob didn't yet exist. Any father who is reading this book can recall the phase of life—perhaps it was a more carefree era!—prior to begetting their firstborn child. It is the nature of offspring not to exist . . . until they do.

Since Arius was something of a biblical literalist, he took this chronological idea and applied it to God's Son as well. The only begotten Son of God must have sprung into being when God decided to make the world. This goes beyond

Tertullian's idea that the Second Person's sonship began for the sake of creation, for Tertullian at least accepted the eternality of the Word before he became a Son. But for Arius, a key slogan captured his more radical view: "There was when he was not." In other words, there was a time—a long time, in fact—when the Second Person didn't yet exist.

Arius's followers in Alexandria incorporated this slogan into their everyday conversation, so that it became a rallying cry for their neighborhood faction. Arius even composed doctrinal songs in a popular meter to be sung by travelers, workers, and barroom drinkers. We can imagine a shout of "There was when he was not!" arising in an Egyptian tavern as thirsty cowboys guzzled their sludgy beer through reed straws.[2]

The Arians[3] believed the Son was a creature made by God. He was created out of nonbeing, just like the world was created from nothing as well. Having a moment of creation meant the Son couldn't be fully divine or "true God"—for, by definition, God is an eternal being who has no source or origin. The Son must be a lesser being, a glorious creature, yet not God himself. As a creature, the Son couldn't see God perfectly. Nor did he know all things. He even had free will, including the ability to sin, though by great moral effort he managed to refrain from evil. This was the Arian view of Jesus Christ.[4]

The Church Responds

As Arius's ideas took root in Alexandria and began to spread throughout the Nile Delta and other parts of Africa, Bishop Alexander had no choice but to respond in dramatic fashion. Since he was described as "gentle and peaceful" by nature, he tried at first to reason with Arius and help him come to a more moderate view.[5] The bishop believed it was wiser to bring someone back to the truth by persuasion than by force. Alexander arranged for a public disputation in which both sides could present their views while he and some other clergymen listened. But as so often happens on such occasions, no consensus was reached. Each side only doubled down on their view and claimed victory. Unwilling to give up, Alexander held a second disputation, but this one failed to reach a conclusion as well.

At last, Alexander was forced to adjudicate the matter. Siding against Arius, he took his stand with the more traditional view that the Father and Son are coeternal. In particular, Alexander sided with the view of his esteemed predecessor, Origen, who taught the doctrine of eternal generation. The Son has always been sourced in the Father—not chronologically, but timelessly, like a fountain ever welling up from its source. There was never a time when the Son did not exist.

Bishop Alexander commanded Arius to recant his views, but the haughty presbyter refused. Now Alexander had no choice but to excommunicate Arius for heresy. Though Arius departed the city, he left behind a church split. His followers, the Arians, included not only some senior churchmen but many of the common people. Some of them sided with Arius because they believed his doctrines were true, while others thought he had been unjustly excommunicated. A schism had ruptured the Alexandrian church. But the division in Egypt wasn't the worst problem. Like a cancerous tumor, Arius's erroneous doctrines began to send dangerous tendrils into other parts of the empire.

The Spread of Arianism

Arius migrated to the land now called Israel (it was called Syrian Palestine in those days), where he gained support among the local bishops and his ideas found traction. It's hard to say why this area was receptive to his views. Generally speaking, the thinkers of this region preferred the Christology from below. They favored theologies that didn't exalt Christ so high that he lost touch with the created realm. With its creaturely Christ, Arianism might have sounded like a good fit.

But equally likely, it could have been a case of ecclesiastical rivalry. The cities of Roman Palestine and Syria had always felt a sense of competition with the wealthy, intellectual metropolis of Alexandria, especially at the rival city of Antioch. In fact, Arius had been previously trained under a famous Antiochian teacher named Lucian. Perhaps the Syro-Palestinian Christians felt like one of their own had come home after being wrongly accused by the snooty Alexandrians. By seeming to take a stand against Sabellianism, Arius might have been perceived as a heroic guardian of sound doctrine. It would be like a pastor today getting kicked out of New York City for what appeared to be conservative ideas. If those elite New Yorkers didn't like a certain set of doctrines, that might be just enough reason for conservative Christians of Atlanta or Dallas to adopt them with gusto.

In any case, the Arian point of view spread widely in the eastern Mediterranean region. A group of bishops from as far away as modern-day Turkey convened a synod that declared Arius not guilty of heresy. Letters were dispatched asking everyone to have fellowship with him. Arius even requested and was granted a new church. Since he had been a presbyter in Egypt, he claimed he ought to be allowed to continue in pastoral work. Other key leaders agreed that his view of Christ shouldn't exclude him from ministry.

Back in Egypt, Bishop Alexander found himself forced to write a circular letter of his own. Though he was receiving pressure to reconcile, the bishop couldn't pretend that this was just some trivial point of doctrine. A believer could have a variety of theological views and still be in good standing with the church. Variance on minor points had always been the norm. But no Christian—certainly no pastor!—should call the Son of God an inferior creature with the potential to sin. Arius couldn't preach that from his pulpit and expect to go without chastisement. Alexander penned a strongly worded letter that said:

> To our beloved and most honored fellow-ministers of the catholic church everywhere, Alexander sends greeting in the Lord. Inasmuch as the catholic church is one body and we are commanded in the holy Scriptures to maintain "the bond of unity and peace" (Ephesians 4:3), it is fitting to write and mutually acquaint one another with the condition of things among each of us, in order that "if one member suffers or rejoices, we may either sympathize with each other or rejoice together" (1 Corinthians 12:26). Know therefore that there have recently arisen in our diocese lawless and anti-Christian men teaching apostasy which one may justly consider and call the forerunner of Antichrist. I truly wished to consign this disorder to silence, so that if possible the evil might be confined to the apostates alone and not go forth into other districts and contaminate the ears of some of the simple believers . . . [But because of their widespread heresy], these men have been publicly repudiated by the church and condemned. We are indeed grieved on account of the lostness of these persons, especially so because, after having been previously instructed in the doctrines of the church, they have now apostatized from them.[6]

In Alexander's forthright letter to his fellow churchmen, he singled out for criticism one bishop in particular. Alexander rebuked him sharply for siding with Arius. This chastised bishop was especially prominent, having many friends who were inclined to agree with whatever he said. His name was

Eusebius—not the more well-known Eusebius who penned the first work of church history (although that Eusebius also sided with Arius for a time), but a second Eusebius, one with a great deal of ecclesiastical power. Somehow, this second Eusebius had managed to finagle an episcopal transfer from his home city of Beirut to the prominent city of Nicomedia. When he saw his name in Alexander's circular letter, Eusebius of Nicomedia decided to go to war against his opponent down in Egypt.

Theology Meets Politics

Today, the city of Nicomedia isn't all that famous. It is the fairly nondescript town of Izmit in Turkey, a port on the Sea of Marmara. But at the time when Eusebius was its bishop, Nicomedia was one of the empire's foremost cities. Why? Because for strategic regions, the emperor Diocletian had designated it as one of his imperial capitals. In this historical era, the government was no longer administered out of Rome, which was too far from various frontier bases that could more ably defend the empire's borders against barbarian incursions. Nicomedia had assumed important status after Diocletian built an imperial palace there. The emperor realized his army could be quickly deployed against any nearby threat. Likewise, the secure harbor could send out ships against the Gothic hordes on the other side of the Black Sea.

The emperor reigning from Nicomedia in the early 320s, however, wasn't Diocletian. It was Licinius, a previous friend to Christians who had recently started persecuting them again, banning their assemblies and even putting some of their leaders to death. Bishop Eusebius managed to escape that fate by currying favor with the emperor's queen. Flavia Julia Constantia was sympathetic to Christianity, so

Eusebius grew powerful by having her ear in all matters religious. Because of this strategic position, Eusebius was one of the most influential bishops in the Christian world.

But by the year 324, things were about to change. Constantia's powerful brother had previously been allied with Licinius. Recently, though, they'd fallen into a dispute over sovereign boundaries. Now the queen's brother was mobilizing a massive army and a fleet of warships to advance on his brother-in-law in Nicomedia. Everyone knew a civil war had just started whose outcome would leave only one man standing. Though Licinius might win by relying on the pagan gods, it was whispered across the empire that the Supreme God of Christianity favored his opponent. That man's name was Constantine—and his troops were marching behind a mighty banner that bore the emblem of a cross. Only time would tell whether Jupiter or Jesus would claim the ultimate allegiance of Rome.

Part 3

Nicene Christianity

9

Constantine's Council

Nicaea, 325

When giving an account of the Nicene Creed as this book attempts to do, some attention must be devoted to politics in addition to theology. Not everything at Nicaea hinged on intellectual ideas or scriptural exegesis. It wasn't simply a case of wise bishops huddled over their Bibles, debating verses until a final vote was taken and a creed was drafted. As with any major event in world history, the motivations were complex. In an age when nobody believed in the separation of religion from government, it was inevitable that the political sphere would influence the outcome of the Council of Nicaea.

And what were the politics of those days? We have already mentioned Diocletian, but let's go into more detail. Several decades before the council, in 284, this skillful emperor had split the empire into four quadrants. Two would be ruled by senior emperors and two by junior men who would eventually rise to occupy the top spots. Historians refer to this arrangement as the tetrarchy, which means "rule by four." Unfortunately, it was an unstable scenario that led to a lot of civil war. Various claimants fought to get into the tetrarchy, or to defeat one another once they had gotten in. Many tetrarchs came and went as the struggles and battles unfolded.

Forty years later, only two men had survived in power: Constantine in the West and his brother-in-law, Licinius, in the East. As we saw in the last chapter, those two rulers were locked in a conflict whose resolution would end the tetrarchy and restore singular rulership over the Roman Empire.

The course of their war need not concern us here, only the outcome. Constantine's son, Crispus, scored some major naval victories that put Licinius on the run. He retreated to Chrysopolis, where his army was routed in the autumn of 324. By the time Constantine caught up with Licinius, he was cowering in Nicomedia with no soldiers left. After Queen Constantia pleaded with her brother for her husband's life, Constantine agreed not to execute Licinius but only send him into exile.[1] Now Constantine found himself, like the great emperors before him, the sole ruler of Rome's vast dominions.

Yet unlike the greats such as Augustus, Hadrian, or Trajan, Emperor Constantine had a very different idea about how to unify his realm. All the previous emperors had used pagan religion as the glue that held the empire together. But not Constantine. He had scored an earlier victory—the famous Battle of the Milvian Bridge in 312—by choosing to mark his soldiers' shields and war banners with a Christian cross.[2] He did this after he witnessed a bright vision in the sky in which a crisscrossed shape informed him that he should "conquer by this." The heavenly omen was followed by a dream in which Jesus (so it was believed) commanded the emperor to make a military standard that incorporated the sign.

Constantine's spiritual journey is a complex topic that historians have loved to debate. When did the conversion actually happen? Was it authentic or contrived for the sake of political expediency?[3] Whatever the case, there can be no question that in 324, Constantine had every intention of supporting the bishops of the Christian church. Their steadfast unity in the face of persecution during the previous two decades had given Christianity a cohesiveness that polytheism just didn't have. "One God, one Lord, one church, and one emperor"—that seemed like a winning formula to Constantine. But right then, at the very moment of his supposed victory through Jesus, Constantine got word of the church split between Alexander and Arius.

Imperial Intervention

Immediately, the emperor wrote a sharply worded letter to the two disputants. It's worth quoting at length because it reveals how badly Constantine wanted unity in his realm. He said:

> Not long ago I visited Nicomedia, and had intended to proceed immediately from that city to the East. It was while I was hurrying towards you [in Alexandria], and had already finished the greater part of the journey [by reaching Antioch], that the news of this matter reversed my plan, so that I would not be forced to see with my own eyes that which I felt myself scarcely able even to hear.[4]

So disturbed was the emperor upon learning of the dreadful quarrel in Egypt that he immediately retreated home. From Nicomedia, he sent the letter that criticized both Alexander and Arius for stirring up needless dissension in the church. Constantine explained,

> So when I found that an intolerable spirit of mad folly had overcome the whole of Africa, through the influence of those

117

who with heedless frivolity had presumed to divide the religion of the people into diverse sects, I was anxious to stop the course of this disorder. . . . And yet, now that I have made a careful inquiry into the origin and foundation of these differences, I have found the cause to be of a truly insignificant character, and quite unworthy of such fierce contention. . . . As far, then, as regards Divine Providence, let there be one faith, and one understanding among you, one united judgment concerning God. . . . But as to your subtle disputations on questions of little or no significance, though you may be unable to harmonize in opinion, such differences should be confined to your own private minds and thoughts.[5]

To enforce the emperor's will, Constantine dispatched his foremost Christian adviser, a distinguished Spanish bishop named Ossius, to negotiate a resolution at Alexandria. Unfortunately, Ossius's mission failed, and the two sides couldn't come to an agreement. Now what? How would the first Christian emperor resolve this feud that threatened societal discord just as he was trying to reunite his realm like in the days of old?

Constantine's Council at Nicaea

In January or February of 325, some unrelated church matters required a council at Antioch. About sixty bishops made their way to that city. As Ossius returned to Nicomedia after his failure in Egypt, he stopped at Antioch and made sure the Arian problem formed part of the council's discussions. After some debate, the overwhelming majority vindicated the theology held by Alexander and sharply criticized Arian ideas as newfangled and unbiblical. The Christian church, said Ossius and his fellow council members, had never viewed Jesus as one of God's creatures.

Three men at the council were singled out for holding this blasphemous view. Among them was Eusebius of Caesarea, who would later publish his famous *Church History* in multiple volumes. The three Arian sympathizers were excommunicated for not adhering to true doctrine. However, an opportunity to repent was granted to them. Another council, one even more "magnificent and sacred," would be held that summer at Ancyra, which is today the capital of Turkey in the interior of that nation.[6] The summertime gathering would adjudicate once and for all the issue of Christ's deity.

The location of Nicaea.

At some point, though, Emperor Constantine got word of this upcoming council and decided to relocate it. Why? He gave three reasons: the superior climate at Nicaea, its proximity to the coast for those arriving by sea, and its closeness to Nicomedia, the imperial capital. No doubt, the emperor didn't want to hold the council at Nicomedia itself, lest it come under the sway of its powerful Arian bishop, the other Eusebius. Yet neither did Constantine want it to be held at distant Ancyra, where a powerful anti-Arian bishop named Marcellus presided. Nicaea—the city of *nike* or "victory"—seemed like a perfect compromise in terms of climate, accessibility, and, most importantly, a nonpartisan theological outlook.

Immediately, the emperor dispatched letters across his realm with very generous terms. All prominent bishops throughout the empire were invited to attend the council at full imperial expense. Their travel costs would be covered by the government, either by supplying them with pack animals or allowing them to use the imperial transit system of inns stationed a day's journey apart. This superior mode of

Iznik, Turkey. Photo by Omerograf (Wikimedia Commons, CC BY-SA 4.0).

travel was normally reserved for high-ranking dignitaries, key military officials, and speedy messengers. Now the persecuted pastors of the Christian church were being treated like personal friends of the emperor.

Over the course of the late spring months, about three hundred bishops made their way to Nicaea, each bringing a small retinue of helpers.[7] Modern scholars estimate the total number of visitors to have been around 1,200 to 1,900 people. Probably they lodged in private homes or perhaps in tents. Most of them were from the eastern part of the empire: Greece, Asia Minor, Syro-Palestine, and Egypt. Yet a few guests were Latin-speakers from the western parts of the realm: Italy, Spain, Gaul, and North Africa. Pope Sylvester of Rome couldn't attend personally, so he sent two theologians, Vitus and Vincentius, to represent him. Even one bishop from the far eastern territory of Persia attended the big event. Ossius of Spain chaired the proceedings. In this way, the council was truly ecumenical, or worldwide, though it was heavily skewed toward the Greek-speaking half of the Roman Empire.

We don't know many details about the council's business, nor even its precise venue. The building that hosted the proceedings is simply called a "palace" in Nicaea, a spot whose exact location is unknown today. In the Middle Ages, the palace reception hall was turned into the Church of the Holy Fathers near the city's northern gate. Unfortunately, that building has been lost to the ravages of time, earthquakes, and Muslim invasions. Probably its ruins lie beneath some nondescript shops or houses in modern Iznik.

Our best source for what took place at the council is Eusebius of Caesarea (who was there to vindicate his name against charges of false doctrine). He describes the magnificent opening session in which Constantine entered the hall in his best regalia. Eusebius states that upon a certain signal, everyone rose to their feet. The emperor walked between the bishops "like some heavenly angel of God, his bright mantle shedding lustre like beams of light, shining with the fiery radiance of a purple robe, and decorated with the dazzling brilliance of gold and precious stones."[8]

Upon reaching the far end of the hall, the emperor asked permission to join them, and the bishops agreed. Only after they said yes did Constantine take a seat, followed by the crowd. Don't miss what Constantine was doing here. He was giving full imperial dignity to Christianity in the same way that pagan religion used to receive it, while at the same time humbling himself as a mere layman in the presence of clergy. Something very big was happening to the status of the Christian church in the public sphere. The bishops could only marvel at what they were seeing.

And what a mangled lot these bishops were! Emperor Diocletian had started the Great Persecution against the church in 303. Constantine had only partly been able to deflect its bloodshed and tortures in his parts of the empire. One ancient historian describes the attendees at the Council of Nicaea this way:

> Many, just like the holy apostle [Paul], bore in their bodies the marks of the Lord Jesus Christ (Galatians 6:17). . . . Paul, bishop of Neo-Caesarea, a fortress situated on the banks of the Euphrates, had suffered from the frantic rage of Licinius. He had been deprived of the use of both hands by the application of a red-hot iron, by which the nerves which give motion to the muscles had been contracted and rendered dead. Some had had their right eye dug out, others had lost their right arm. Among these was Paphnutius of Egypt. In short, the council looked like an assembled army of martyrs.[9]

Imagine these godly bishops—blinded, twisted, maimed, and scarred—now being asked by the emperor whether he might sit among them. These men who had known the horrors of dark dungeons and suffocating mines were now the honored guests of the world's greatest monarch. There could be no question that Nicaea was a city of victory!

The Creed of Nicaea (325)

Over the course of June and July, the bishops wrestled with the Trinitarian issues under dispute (along with a host of other important ecclesiastical matters that needed addressing at this worldwide council). Eusebius of Caesarea informs us that his Arian-leaning view was exonerated—but this was only because he fudged the terms and privately interpreted some of the creed's words in ways that he preferred. As Eusebius tells it, he put forward as a starting point his hometown baptismal creed from Caesarea, the very city where Peter had converted Cornelius the centurion and Paul had made a defense of his faith in the book of Acts. This coastal city had been constructed by King Herod the Great. Over the years, it had become a leading Christian center, housing the ancient church's greatest library. These records provided the substance of what went into Eusebius's *Church History*. However, modern scholars who study creeds do not believe that Eusebius's version formed the basis of the one at Nicaea. Instead, the council members drafted their own version that used traditional creedal statements yet added some key terms.

The most important terminological addition was the Greek word *homoousios* to describe the relationship of the Father and Son. It meant "same substance." The Latin-based version of the word, which we still use in English today, is "consubstantial." This was a term that no Arian could accept, a line in the sand they couldn't cross. While many of the traditional, biblical expressions could be twisted to have the meaning the Arians desired—for example, "firstborn of all creation" in Colossians 1:15 could be used to support Christ's creaturely status—the word *homoousios* definitively ruled out the Arian view. If the Father and Son were consubstantial, sharing the very same substance, then one couldn't exist when the other didn't. If substance is shared between two entities, so is their timeline. If A and B have the same essence, there can be no time when A existed without B. Once the term *homoousios* was inserted in the creed of Nicaea, the Arian view was automatically excluded.

Just to make sure this was clear, the creed included some specific "anathemas" at the end—that is, condemnations of false doctrines. The creed declared that if anyone held "There was when he was not" (the notorious Arian slogan)

First Council of Nicaea by Michael Damaskinos, 1591.

or taught that the Son was created out of nothing or could change (i.e., fall into sin), that person stood condemned by the worldwide Christian church. Arius was excommunicated along with two other bishops from Libya. All the rest of the council fathers—including Saint Nicholas of Myra, who much later became the basis for the Santa Claus legends[10]— signed an affirmation of the creed. Even the two Eusebiuses, the bishops of Nicomedia and Caesarea, signed the document, though they privately kept their own interpretation of the creedal words that were intended to exclude them.

With all these issues resolved, everyone went up to Nicomedia for a big party to celebrate Constantine's twentieth year of reign. (Though he had only recently become the sole emperor, he had been crowned as a partial emperor two decades earlier and this occasion marked that anniversary.) The historian Eusebius records—probably with some of his usual exaggeration—that "not one bishop" was missing from the festivities. He notes that a great banquet was laid out for the guests, guarded by rows of soldiers between whom the bishops passed "fearlessly." Many of those limping men would have had reason to fear imperial soldiers only a few years before. Now they were being seated at the emperor's table.

Eusebius goes on to declare that this momentous event "might have been supposed [to be] an imaginary representation of the kingdom of Christ, and that what was happening was a 'dream, not fact.'"[11] Surely, some of those bishops must have felt like they were dreaming. They could hardly believe how one man, the first Christian emperor, had so drastically changed the church's lot from bloody persecution to imperial favor. The highest authority on earth had supported the biblical doctrine that God and Jesus are coeternal and consubstantial. The future looked bright for the Christian church. But as the coming decades would soon reveal, those banqueting bishops weren't as unified as they seemed.

10

The Debate Rages On, Part 1

Consubstantial, Similar, or Dissimilar?

Sometimes in warfare, two steps forward are followed by three steps back. Historians tell us the trench warfare of World War I was like that. Soldiers captured precious ground through blood, sweat, and tears, then lost it shortly thereafter. The back-and-forth combat resulted in a hard stalemate. Only the long story would identify the eventual victors.

Despite Nicaea being the city of victory, the theological warfare in the years between 325 and 381 followed the same pattern. The ground that Alexander's party had seemed to capture so decisively at the council fell into Arian hands during the ensuing years. Scottish historian Sara Parvis remarks that "if we focus on the reception of the Council of Nicaea, the progress of events is fairly clear. The key acts of the council were all one by one reversed over these years."[1] Though the defenders of *homoousios* won big in 325, things quickly changed. It soon looked like future Christians would be worshiping a creaturely Christ instead of an eternal one. The middle decades of the fourth century were a precarious time for the ancient church!

Traditionally, the theological view taught by the followers of Arius has been called "Arianism." Though we'll use the term in this book for simplicity's sake, it isn't a very accurate expression. As it turns out, Arius wasn't a key player in the decades after the Nicene council condemned him. Not many people wanted to claim his legacy, so he gradually disappeared off the scene.

One thing we do hear about Arius is the embarrassing nature of his death. When he was in Constantinople one day, near the Column of Constantine whose pedestal and pillar can still be seen in modern Istanbul, he felt the need to visit a public lavatory. There, according to several ancient accounts, he suffered explosive gastrointestinal distress and his rectum fell out, along with blood and other organs, so that he immediately died. Over the years, ancient people used to whisper and point to the latrine as the place where the arch-heretic met his gory fate. The implications of the story are obvious: Such a shameful death must reflect God's poor estimation of the man. One writer even compared Arius to the biblical traitor Judas, who "burst open in the middle and all his bowels gushed out" (Acts 1:18).[2]

Today's scholars don't like to use the term "Arian" to describe the theologians of the mid-fourth century who rejected the creed of 325. Not only did they never take up the mantle of Arius as some kind of heroic founder but they also held positions that differed from his in small yet significant ways. Those differences meant they often differed from one another as well. Theologically speaking, they can't be lumped together as a cohesive unit. The only thing they had in common was their rejection of *homoousios* as the proper descriptor for the Son's relation to the Father.

Yet it was precisely this commonality that caused one of the church's finest theologians to view them as a single enemy, a multiheaded Hydra that in reality was just one devilish foe. This man was Athanasius of Alexandria, a staunch defender of Nicene orthodoxy and the person most responsible for its eventual triumph. Despite his flaws—traits like stubbornness, inflexibility, and a willingness to use hard rhetoric and power politics—Athanasius remains one of the greatest heroes of church history. He is yet another African who helped to forge the doctrine of the Trinity. It's time to meet this little man who had such a big impact on the Christian faith.

Athanasius Against the World

An ancient account tells us that Bishop Alexander was visiting a seashore location one day when he observed something amusing.[3] As some boys were playing on the beach, they started imitating the things done in a church. For a while, the stately bishop watched the boys as they marched around and made sacred gestures. But then one of them started using water to do "more secret and sacramental things" to the others. Concerned, the bishop summoned his fellow clergymen to observe the proceedings. Finally, he made some of them fetch the boys and bring them before him.

"Were you performing a baptism?" he asked the frightened children.

Icon of Athanasius of Alexandria.

At first, they wouldn't answer, but eventually they acknowledged the truth: Yes, in their game, one of them was baptizing the others. The bishop asked the baptized boys if they were Christian catechumens—that is, actual candidates for baptism. They were. Next, he asked the ringleader what he had said during the ceremony. It turned out he had recited the baptismal liturgy with precision. He had asked all the official questions, and the boys had given proper responses.

Now Alexander conferred with his clergy. After some deliberation, he turned back to the boys. "That ceremony counts as a legitimate baptism," he announced. "You boys are baptized Christians." Turning to the ringleader, he asked, "What is your name?"

"Athanasius," said the little brown-skinned child. Clearly, he was a Copt—a native Egyptian, not a Greek.

"Athanasius, I am going to talk to your parents," the bishop informed him. "If they agree, you shall be raised for church service, like Samuel in the days of old."

Since Athanasius's parents were delighted with the idea, the boy received a formal education that culminated in young adulthood with biblical and theological studies. Athanasius grew up at Alexander's side, attended the Council of Nicaea along with his master—where it is reported that he gave important theological guidance despite his youth—and eventually succeeded Alexander as the bishop of the empire's second greatest city. Athanasius was chosen for this honor despite not having attained the required age of thirty. Clearly, he was a young man with a lot of promise.

Bishop Athanasius found himself the primary carrier of the Nicene flag in the decades when its ideas were under full-blown assault. Though Emperor Constantine had supported the creed of 325 with its *homoousios* clause, for political reasons—not least, the influence of the Arian bishop, Eusebius of Nicomedia—other factions began to gain ground.

They petitioned to have Arius reinstated into church fellowship, and this request succeeded. They also demanded that he be granted admittance to the communion table in Constantinople. It was while Arius was on his way to church that he experienced his deadly bathroom "accident"—though some historians have suggested human poison was the cause, not God's judgment. In any case, Constantine had proven himself unwilling to come down on one theological position over another. He was committed to church unity in whatever form it took. For the rest of his reign, he tried to heal the divisions by taking a middle ground approach. Constantine even allowed Eusebius of Nicomedia to preside over his baptism, which he received shortly before his death in 337.

Constantine's three sons who succeeded him were at odds in their Trinitarian allegiances. Although two of them generally supported Athanasius, they didn't have the power to make Nicene Trinitarianism the law of the land. The third of them, Constantius II, was actively hostile to it. He openly sided with one of the Arian perspectives—which meant he and Athanasius would be mortal enemies. The feisty bishop also opposed later emperors such as Valens, who likewise identified with Arianism, and Julian the Apostate, the only post-Constantinian emperor to reject any form of Christianity and try to return the empire to paganism. Athanasius had many adversaries in high places!

Because of all the political intrigue that went along with the theological wrangling, Athanasius was kicked out of his Alexandrian church five different times. The emperors either commanded that he leave, or local threats made it too dangerous for him to stay. Sometimes, he managed to escape to the Egyptian countryside or the remote deserts of the Upper Nile, where the ascetic monks took him in and gave him shelter. Other times, Athanasius was exiled all the way to the western empire, to Rome—where Pope Julius loved him and agreed with his Nicene theology—or even as far away as Trier in Germany.

Athanasius being gone from his church or under duress gave Arianism the freedom to gain more ground. One eyewitness of those times, the great biblical scholar Jerome, remarked that despite the seeming victory at Nicaea, a few years later, Arianism had triumphed in its place. When an Arian creed was published at another council as an attempted replacement for the one from 325, Jerome could scarcely believe it. "The Nicene Faith stood condemned by acclamation," he lamented. "The whole world groaned, and was astonished to find itself Arian."[4]

For many years, Bishop Athanasius represented a lone voice striving to preserve the doctrine of the Trinity against those who would water it down by making Christ in some way inferior to his Father. Historian Sara Parvis insists that "the case for Nicaea was held together above all by one man, Athanasius of Alexandria. . . . Without Athanasius's political and theological understanding of the importance of that first 'great and holy Council,' and his rhetorical skill in communicating it, the Creed of Nicaea and the term *homoousios* alike would almost certainly have sunk with very little trace long before 381."[5]

Despite such fierce opposition from every direction, Athanasius took his stand on the full deity of Christ and would not budge. Because of his dogged determination to defend the Trinity, church history has described him with the slogan *Athanasius contra mundum*.[6] This Latin phrase means "Athanasius against the world"—and in a very real sense, during the middle decades of the fourth century, that was true. Almost everyone had taken up a different view from Nicaea. What were those erroneous views? And how did the true one finally prevail?

Consubstantial, Similar, or Dissimilar?

We have already seen how the creed of 325 put forth the word *homoousios*, or "consubstantial," to designate the Son's equal deity and eternality with the Father. But what words did the various Arians prefer? Although there were almost as many views as there were bishops to hold them, each with slightly different nuances, two words (or, actually, prefixes) marked out the main theological trajectories in the years between 325 and 381.

First, some theologians adopted the term *homoiousios*. Look closely at what you just read. It's not the same as *homoousios*. Do you see the extra *i*? The prefix *homo-* means "same," and *ousia* means "essence" or "substance." Identity of substance was the Nicene view held by Athanasius. But when you add the Greek letter *iota*, it becomes *homoi-*, or "similar." These theologians said the Son was "similar" to the Father, but they left open the possibility that in fundamental ways, he might fall short of the Father's deity. The Son might be a second-level being, which the defenders of Nicaea couldn't accept.

Today, when people want to describe something as minor, they say, "It does not make one iota of difference." But here was a case where the Greek *iota* made all the difference in the world! Jesus himself recognized that the smallest Greek letter could change everything when he said, "Until heaven and earth pass away, not an iota, not a dot, will pass from the Law until all is accomplished" (Matt. 5:18). When it comes to the Trinity, the Son of God cannot be similar (*homoi-*) to the Father. He must share the Father's very same (*homo-*) essence or substance.

The other important prefix was *anomoi-*, or "dissimilar." Those who held this doctrine taught that the Son's dissimilarity meant he was a creation of the Father, just like Arius had originally said. But whereas Arius claimed the Son was created out of nothing, the Anomoeans were willing to say the Son was created out of the Father's self. Even so, the Son wasn't eternal, which meant he was inferior to the heavenly Father.

Here's the bottom line. The essential division between Nicene Trinitarianism and any type of Arianism hinges on this question: Does the Son share equally in the deity of the Father? If the two of them are consubstantial and coeternal, as Athanasius and the creed of Nicaea insisted, it means their deity is entirely equal. But if the Son is only "similar" to the Father, or perhaps even "dissimilar," it demotes the Son's deity, so he falls short of being fully God. While a glorified creature could serve as a moral example in a system of works salvation, a grace-based gospel requires the Son's full deity. Athanasius and the Nicene party stood firm on their belief—against the whole world, when necessary—that the biblical gospel proclaims a Savior who is God in the flesh, come down to us for the sake of our salvation. The full impact of the Son's descent can only be appreciated when we recognize how far he came: *all the way* from the place of equality with God (Phil. 2:6–11).

Perhaps as you reflect on these theological tussles, you might think, "What about the Holy Spirit? Didn't the ancients care about him?" After all, this dispute was about the Trinity—the three persons of the Godhead. The First and Second Persons were being discussed in minute detail. Didn't the church fathers debate about the Third Person as well?

They certainly did! Although the original controversy was sparked by consideration of the Son's relationship to the Father, in the late fourth century, the doctrine of the Spirit (called "pneumatology") was put on the table as well. To continue the legacy of Athanasius, three mighty theologians rose up to help him carry the Nicene banner. Since they were from the same region in Asia Minor, they are known as the Three Cappadocians. After their theological labors took root, the Roman Empire was finally ready to call a second great council in 381 and cast its lot with the Nicene view of the Trinity.

11

The Debate Rages On, Part 2

Is the Holy Spirit Divine?

T he creed of Nicaea arose out of a specific circumstance: the need to refute Arius's claim that the Son had been created by God. The whole empire had taken up the topic of the Son's relationship to the Father. One observer who lived in those theologically inquisitive times put it this way:

All the affairs of the city are full of this stuff! The narrow lanes, the markets, the wide avenues, and the neighborhood streets! The clothing hucksters, the moneychangers, and those who sell us food! If you ask someone for change, he philosophizes to you about the Begotten and the Unbegotten. If you inquire about the price of a loaf, the answer is, "The Father is greater, and the Son is subordinate." If you ask, "Is the bath ready?" the guy asserts that the Son is derived out of non-being.[1]

In other words, everyone was discussing Trinitarian theology—even the common folk. However, the conversations centered on how the Second Person related to the First. The Holy Spirit wasn't yet part of the discussion.

This becomes especially obvious when we read Nicaea's creed of 325 in its entirety. Although there isn't an official English translation, a good one appears in the book *The Creeds of Christendom* by church historian Philip Schaff. It runs as follows, in three Trinitarian articles plus the "anathemas" (condemnations):

> We believe in one God, the Father Almighty, Maker of all things visible and invisible.
>
> And in one Lord Jesus Christ, the Son of God, begotten of the Father, the only-begotten; that is, of the essence of the Father, God of God, Light of Light, very God of very God, begotten, not made, being of one substance [*homoousion*] with the Father; by whom all things were made, both in heaven and on earth; who for us men, and for our salvation, came down and was incarnate and was made man; he suffered, and the third day he rose again, ascended into heaven; from thence he shall come to judge the quick and the dead.
>
> And in the Holy Ghost.
>
> But those who say: "There was a time when he was not"; and "He was not before he was made"; and "He was made out of nothing," or "He is of another substance" or "essence," or "The Son of God is created," or "changeable," or "alterable"—they are condemned by the holy catholic and apostolic church.[2]

Obviously, a creed like this would be hard to recite today with those clunky anathemas that have a specific, technical focus. This was partly why a later creed was deemed necessary in 381—a story we will address in the next chapter. But apart from the unpleasant curses at the end, another remarkable aspect of the creed is its theological imbalance. It says little about the Father, who is simply identified as

Icon of Emperor Constantine and the council fathers
holding the Creed of Nicaea (325). The word *homoousios*
appears in the fifth line.

the almighty Creator. The Son receives the majority of the
attention: the nature of his begetting, his consubstantiality with the Father, and his cosmic story of incarnation,
crucifixion, resurrection, ascension, and eventual return.
Then what is said about the Holy Spirit? Virtually nothing!
Mere belief in the Spirit's existence is confessed without
any specific pneumatology to explain who he is or what
he does.

The creed of 325 exhibits a firm awareness of God's
threefold identity, yet retains some lingering uncertainty
about the Third Person. Earlier in this book, we saw
how Old Testament Israel understood that the one God

extended himself into the world through his Word and Breath. Although the Israelites or Jews didn't use a specific threefold depiction of God, his triplicate existence became clear with the advent of Jesus and the publication of the New Testament. In particular, the Lord's baptismal formula stamped the triune name on the Christian mind: "Go therefore and make disciples of all nations, baptizing them in the name of the Father and of the Son and of the Holy Spirit" (Matt. 28:19). In addition, the apostle Paul's benediction gave Christians a Trinitarian mindset: "The grace of the Lord Jesus Christ and the love of God and the fellowship of the Holy Spirit be with you all" (2 Cor. 13:14).

After the New Testament era, early church attempts to make sense of the Third Person didn't always get things right. Modalism, for example, viewed the Spirit as just one mode of divine self-expression, not a distinct person in his own right. Others viewed the Spirit as a kind of vague, mystical energy or the empowering presence of God. Then, in the mid–third century, Origen really got it wrong—one of his more "horrid" moments—when he declared the Holy Spirit to be an exalted creature made by God. This notion grew out of some earlier theories that the Spirit was a type of angel.

By the dawn of the fourth century, confusion still reigned. When Arius threw the church into a tumult with his creaturely Christ, all the theological attention pivoted to Christology as the Nicenes rebutted Arius, while the Arians rushed to his defense. But starting around 360, the Nicene party realized that they also needed to deal with pneumatology. Some Arian sympathizers were continuing the view of Origen by teaching the creaturely status of the Holy Spirit. With the orthodox, Nicene response to this problematic trajectory, a full-fledged doctrine of the Trinity at last began to take shape.

The Three Cappadocians

Bishop Athanasius, the courageous yet often lonely torch-bearer of Nicaea, finally received some heavy-duty theological assistance during the last ten years of his life. Two brothers and one of their friends burst onto the church scene, offering their substantial intellectual firepower to the Nicene cause. They were Gregory of Nazianzus (329–390); Basil of Caesarea (330–379); and his younger brother, Gregory of Nyssa (335–395). Because the cities where they ministered were all located in Cappadocia, these three men are often grouped together based on their home region.

We should note that the family of Basil and the second Gregory also produced a prominent sister: Macrina the Younger, a brilliant thinker, yet one known more for her ascetic holiness than for complex Trinitarian theology. All of them were descended from a godly Christian grandmother called Macrina the Elder. Evidently, the central region of Asia Minor was fertile ground for producing great Christian champions at this time! The caves of Cappadocia where ancient monks made their homes can still be visited today. At any rate, down in Egypt, Bishop Athanasius appreciated this newfound source of support.

And it came just in time. A group of non-Nicene theologians had emerged with a problematic doctrine about the Holy Spirit. They are known to history as the Pneumatomachians (pronounced "new-matto-MOCK-ians"), which means the "Spirit Fighters"—not that they fought against the Spirit himself, but only his deity. What did they believe? Their main leaders didn't accept the *homoousios* term from Nicaea. On the other hand, they weren't out-and-out Arians who called

Christ a creature. Instead, they accepted the *homoi-* prefix that allowed Christ to be "similar" to the Father, possessing a lower kind of deity. But when it came to the Holy Spirit, the Pneumatomachians denied his deity altogether. The Spirit was even less similar to God than Christ—a high-level being, yet in the distant third rank. He certainly wasn't to be worshiped or glorified equally with the Father.

The Three Cappadocians took it upon themselves to engage the Spirit Fighters and refute their low view of the Holy Spirit. Along with Athanasius, the Cappadocians articulated a doctrine of the Spirit's full and equal deity to that of the Father and Son. Basil of Caesarea was a little more cautious in his approach. He insisted that the Spirit deserved the same divine honor as the other two persons; the Spirit is on par with them and by no means a creature. Yet Basil thought it wiser to refrain from directly calling the Spirit "God." Instead, the Spirit should be "glorified with the Father and the Son."

Basil's brother, Gregory of Nyssa, went further. He insisted—based on biblical passages such as Psalm 33:6, which speaks of God's Word and Breath—that the three persons were united in their essence. And their friend Gregory of Nazianzus went all the way by identifying the Holy Spirit as God. "What then? Is the Spirit God?" he asked in one of his writings. "Most certainly! Well then, is he consubstantial? Yes, of course, if he is God."[3]

With the efforts of the Three Cappadocians added to the work of Athanasius, the Arians and Spirit Fighters found themselves pushed back in ways they hadn't been for many years. Even when Athanasius died in 373, passing on his bishopric (that is, his ecclesiastic position) to a disciple named Peter, the Cappadocian fathers continued their Trinitarian work. At last, the theological balance seemed to be tipping in favor of Nicaea and the *homoousios* clause. The ecclesiastical world was finally ready to apply this term to all three Trinitarian persons. And at that very moment, as the sovereign timing of God would have it, things were beginning to change in the political realm as well.

Emperor Theodosius: Champion of Nicaea

As the church's leaders debated vital theology, what was happening over in the parallel track of politics? Let's pick up that story where we left off: with the triumph of Emperor Constantine. After defeating Licinius in 324, he had reunited the Roman Empire under himself as a single ruler, then immediately called the Council of Nicaea. In theory, unity had been achieved. Yet theological factions continued, so Constantine tried his hardest to hold them together in one church. He cared primarily about undermining paganism and replacing it with Christianity, not drilling down on minute points of biblical doctrine.

Upon Constantine's death, he divided the realm among his three sons, which reintro-
duced the concept of multiple rule. Though this wasn't a formal tetrarchy, the same situation returned, in which various men claimed authority over different parts of Rome's vast dominions. During the course of the fourth century AD, many figures came and went, sometimes allying with each other, sometimes going to war, but rarely (if ever) standing still. This polarized environment was ripe for factions, both theological and political.

Bust of Theodosius I. Photo by Jona Lendering (Wikimedia Commons, CC BY-SA 4.0).

In the year 379, six years after the death of Athanasius, a man came to power in the eastern half of the empire whose religious policies the Alexandrian bishop surely would have appreciated. Theodosius the Great, the son of a superb general of the same name, was himself trained in the military arts and began his career fighting the Goths who were moving into imperial lands at the time. Contemporary accounts portray him as a strong Christian, but like Constantine before him, today's historians debate how authentic his piety may have been. There are good reasons to think he grew up in Spain in a theologically conservative Christian environment that affirmed the creed of Nicaea as orthodox. So when Emperor Theodosius came to power, that was the kind of Christianity he wanted to see established.

The new emperor immediately published a statement that has come to be called the Edict of Thessalonica. It was addressed to the people of Constantinople, which had been the imperial capital ever since Constantine relocated it there from Nicomedia. Indeed, the name "Constantinople" comes from *Constantinou Polis*, the "City of Constantine." Theodosius intended to take up residence in the capital and from that base spread Nicene Christianity across his realm. His edict from Thessalonica, cosigned by his two fellow emperors, would prepare his subjects for what was to come.

This momentous decree began the process of making Christianity—in the Nicene form held by the bishops of Rome and Alexandria—the official religion of the Roman Empire. Theodosius's edict stated:

> It is Our will that all the peoples who are ruled by the administration of Our Clemency shall practice that religion which the divine Peter the Apostle transmitted to the Romans, as the religion which he introduced makes clear even unto this day. It is evident that this is the religion that is followed by

the Pontiff Damasus [in Rome] and by Peter, Bishop of Alexandria, a man of apostolic sanctity; that is, according to the apostolic disciple and the evangelic doctrine, we shall believe in the single Deity of the Father, the Son, and the Holy Spirit, under the concept of equal majesty and of the Holy Trinity.

We command that those persons who follow this rule shall embrace the name of Catholic Christians.[4] The rest, however, whom We adjudge demented and insane, shall sustain the infamy of heretical dogmas, their meeting places shall not receive the name of churches, and they shall be smitten first by divine vengeance and secondly by the retribution of Our own initiative, which We shall assume in accordance with the divine judgment.[5]

By spearheading such a bold decree in favor of Nicene doctrine, Theodosius no doubt believed he was doing God's will. Immediately, however, the thirty-three-year-old emperor found his faith put to the test when a dreadful illness struck him. As he lay abed in Thessalonica, fearing for his life, he decided he needed to get baptized. Summoning the local bishop, named Ascholius, the dying emperor asked him what version of belief he held. When Ascholius assured him that he "continued to preserve unshaken that faith which from the beginning was delivered by the apostles, and had been confirmed in the Nicene Synod," Theodosius gladly allowed the baptism to proceed.[6] Soon afterward, the sickness departed, and he grew well. Now the young emperor knew what he had to do. Clearly, God's approval of the Nicene faith had been confirmed.

Upon arriving in Constantinople, Theodosius summoned its Arian bishop and asked him to recant. When the man refused, Theodosius banished him, then selected an orthodox substitute: Gregory of Nazianzus, the leader of the Three Cappadocians. He had been teaching the Nicene view of the Trinity from a little house church in the city.[7] Now, with Gregory as the official civic bishop, the churches of the eastern imperial capital would be under the supervision of a staunch Nicene Christian, just like at the great cities of Rome and Alexandria.

Then the emperor went one step further. He issued another decree, which prevented any heretics (the Arians were mentioned by name) from occupying churches or even gathering anywhere inside of a city's walls. Only a believer "who professes the Nicene faith is to be thought of as the genuine worshipper in the Catholic religion," the emperor declared. Such a Christian must confess "God Almighty and Christ his Son in one Name, God from God, Light from Light, [and] . . . not blaspheme the Holy Spirit."[8]

Theodosius's legal pronouncements, combined with his installation of Nicene bishops in strategic churches, tipped the balance away from Arianism and toward the true doctrine of the Trinity. Yet one task remained unfulfilled. Law courts and government edicts couldn't properly explain sound doctrine; only the church could do that. Theodosius understood that while the Council of Nicaea's authority should remain unquestioned, the precise meaning of its creed needed clarification. Not only did it have the awkward anathemas attached to it, the creed also didn't spell out Trinitarian pneumatology with enough specificity. It was time for a second great council to address these matters and entrench Nicene orthodoxy once and for all. In the summer of 381, Theodosius hosted a gathering of churchmen who would bequeath to history the final version of the Nicene Creed that Christians have used ever since, even to the present day.

12

Triumph of the Nicene Creed

Constantinople, 381

According to ancient tradition, 318 church fathers gathered at Nicaea for its council in 325. At Constantinople, five and a half decades later, the number of attendees was half as large, at 150. The later convocation of bishops was also less worldwide than the first. No one came from the western empire, not even from Rome, and some of the Easterners had to leave early. Nevertheless, the Council of Constantinople, summoned by Emperor Theodosius in 381, is considered the second of the seven greatest councils in all of church history. Its creed, officially referred to as the Niceno-Constantinopolitan Creed, is the one that Christians recite today as the "Nicene Creed."

Why is this creed so important? Aside from its accurate Trinitarian theology, it's also the only creed that can claim universal adherence within historic Christianity. After it was put forth at Constantinople, pretty much everyone—at least, everyone who can be considered within the pale of orthodoxy—accepted it. The same can't be said for any other creed. For example, the Apostles' Creed is recited in church services only by Roman Catholics and Protestants, not the Greek Orthodox. The Definition of Chalcedon, a fifth-century clarification about the deity and humanity of Christ, was accepted by those three denominations, but not by certain other ones.[1] During the Reformation period, various statements of faith were composed, such as the Lutheran Augsburg Confession, the Presbyterian Westminster Confession of Faith, and the Anglican Thirty-Nine Articles. Those denominational confessions weren't formally accepted by any other Protestant groups, much less by the Catholics or Orthodox.

In contrast, the universal acceptance of the Nicene Creed stands out as unique. Creedal scholar J. N. D. Kelly observes, "Of all existing creeds it is the only one for which ecumenicity, or universal acceptance, can be plausibly claimed. . . . It is thus one of the few threads by which the tattered fragments of the divided robe of Christendom are held together."[2] How did that come about? What happened at the great council in 381 to seal the deal for the Nicenes and finally unify the Christian world around a single statement of faith?

The Council of Constantinople

Unfortunately, we know even less about the proceedings of the second council than we do the first. No single venue housed the council meetings; apparently it convened in various churches across the eastern capital. Its main, overriding purpose was to reaffirm the faith that had been laid down at Nicaea. Unlike Constantine, who was a brand-new convert and therefore willing to go along with whatever the bishops decided, Theodosius was a lifelong Nicene Christian. That meant he had a specific outcome in mind. He

148

was so starstruck by one of the saintly attendees—Meletius, bishop of Antioch, a steadfast opponent of Arianism—that the young emperor rushed up to him and gazed into his face "like a boy who loves his father."[3] Theodosius then smothered the man in kisses before welcoming all the rest. The council members were invited "to deliberate as was fitting for fathers on the subjects laid before them."[4]

One of the council's first achievements was to confirm the emperor's choice of Gregory of Nazianzus as bishop of Constantinople. The appointment automatically made him the president of the council that had gathered in his city. With such a revered Nicene stalwart in charge of the proceedings, the council's outcome was all but certain.

Meletius of Antioch took great satisfaction in this appointment—but that was the final act of his godly life. The elderly cleric perished for unknown reasons during the summertime meetings. Soon afterward, Gregory asked permission to step down. Many bishops at the council, while acknowledging Gregory's theological brilliance, personal piety, and unimpeachable orthodoxy, nevertheless believed he hadn't been properly installed. One of the church laws enacted at Nicaea was a prohibition against bishops jumping between pastorates in different cities, even for the best of reasons. Rather than cause controversy, Gregory willingly abdicated his new bishopric. Everyone respected his humility. But in truth, he realized he was too much of a reclusive scholar to adequately lead a large urban church with all its heavy burdens. He departed the council before it adjourned, glad to leave behind the intellectual bickering that so often marked such events.

Despite these setbacks, the work of the council went forward. At some point, a creed was put together. The traditional view of its formulation, held through many centuries of church history, claims the new creed was just an

Miniature of the *First Council of Constantinople* in the *Homilies of Gregory of Nazianzus*, Paris Gregory (BnF Grec 510).

expansion of Nicaea's original version. But in modern times, attentive scholars have questioned this. Out of the 178 Greek words in the Nicene Creed, only thirty-three can be attributed to the earlier version from the first council.[5] The word order varies as well. Apparently, the council members at Constantinople used a different confession of faith to put together the second version of the creed.

Or did they? In the late nineteenth and early twentieth centuries, some church historians began to argue that no creed whatsoever had been drawn up at the meeting in 381. How could this be? These historians pointed out that we have no evidence for the rewritten Nicene Creed until seventy years after the council, when a deacon at the famous Council of Chalcedon in 451 read it aloud to enter it into the record as the product of the Constantinopolitan council. Why had no one ever mentioned the new creed during those seventy intervening years? Why didn't it appear in any known liturgy during those decades? Why so much silence, if the creed was so important? The skeptical modern scholars claimed that the Chalcedonian council members must have been mistaken. No creed had been composed during the summer of 381.

In the mid-twentieth century, however, Kelly refuted this thesis. His viewpoint still reigns among contemporary creedal scholars. Theodosius's council did, in fact, formulate a statement of faith. It is identical to the creed recorded in the official acts of the Chalcedonian council, copies of which have survived to the present day. A simple reason explains why no one mentioned it for the first seventy years: Its authors didn't conceive of it as new or different from the original one in 325. The rewritten version was so similar in its main ideas that everyone just assumed it was essentially the same as what had been laid down before. Some clarifications were made, but the inclusion of the *homoousios* clause—the fundamental concept of Nicene Trinitarianism—meant it was really just an elaboration, not a brand-new creed worth mentioning as such. Only with hindsight do we see the importance of the editorial changes. So what were those differences? Perhaps now is the right time to examine them.

The Text of the Nicene Creed

The Council of Constantinople boldly asserted that "The Faith of the 318 Fathers assembled at Nicaea in Bithynia shall not be set aside, but shall remain firm."[6] That was Theodosius's main goal: to reassert Nicene primacy, not to introduce a second creed. Nevertheless, some clarifications needed to be made. As translated in the Anglican *Book of Common Prayer*, the Nicene Creed, in its reformulated or expanded version of 381, reads as follows:

> We believe in one God, the Father, the Almighty, maker of heaven and earth, of all that is, seen and unseen.
>
> We believe in one Lord, Jesus Christ, the only Son of God, eternally begotten of the Father, God from God, Light from Light, true God from true God, begotten, not made, of one Being [*homoousion*] with the Father. Through him all things were made. For us and for our salvation he came down from heaven. By the power of the Holy Spirit he became incarnate from the Virgin Mary, and was made man. For our sake he was crucified under Pontius Pilate; he suffered death and was buried. On the third day he rose again in accordance with the Scriptures; he ascended into heaven and is seated at the right hand of the Father. He will come again in glory to judge the living and the dead, and his kingdom will have no end.
>
> We believe in the Holy Spirit, the Lord, the giver of life, who proceeds from the Father *and the Son*. With the Father and the Son he is worshiped and glorified. He has spoken through the Prophets. We believe in one holy catholic and apostolic church. We acknowledge one baptism for the forgiveness of sins. We look for the resurrection of the dead, and the life of the world to come. Amen.[7]

One of the most obvious differences from the 325 version is the omission of the anathemas at the end. Those curses had arisen in the adversarial and highly polarized context of the first council. But the second council, consisting mostly of already convinced Nicene delegates, didn't feel the need to include any such denunciations. Today's Christians can be grateful for that. Churchgoers who recite creeds want to confess their faith in common with the saints of the ages, not call down divine judgment on heretics.

The Nicene Creed's first article about the Father differs from the 325 version only in its wording, not in its content. Just like before, so here, God the Father is identified as the maker of everything that exists. It is a basic assertion about the Creator God. All ancient creeds began with a statement like this.

The second article on the Son contained more variance from the 325 version. Many of these differences, again, amounted to nuances of wording or noncontroversial expansions. The new references included Christ's crucifixion "under Pontius Pilate," his burial, his resurrection "according to the Scriptures" (1 Corinthians 15:4 NIV), his seat "at the right hand of the Father," and his return "in glory." The claim that the incarnation happened "by the power of the Holy Spirit" and "from the Virgin Mary" was nothing more than a clarification based on Luke's account of the Annunciation in his gospel. These Christological adaptations didn't change anything essential from the original Nicene formula. They were long-standing confessions of the ancient church that appeared often in other baptismal creeds.

Yet there were some substantive changes as well. The assertion in the 325 version that Christ exists "out of the substance [*ousias*] of the Father" was omitted in 381. Probably, this was because the *homoousios* clause already covered that ground, so there was no need to repeat it. Or perhaps the earlier assertion that the Son is "out of" the Father's substance sounded a little bit weaker than stating eternal consubstantiality. A heretic might twist the expression to say the Son was created out of the Father's substance and he didn't exist prior to that creation. Better, thought the council members of 381, to omit the prepositional phrase and let the *homoousios* clause define the situation with clarity.

Another Christological change was the assertion that "his kingdom will have no end." This statement was added to refute a false doctrine held by Marcellus of Ancyra, whose theology possessed modalistic tendencies. Recall that the modalists believed the persons of the Trinity were just different ways of revealing the same being. They said the Son had emerged from the Father as a new revelation of the Godhead, and after him, the Spirit became the next revelation. Some modalists claimed that once the Son was no longer needed, he would retreat back into God and disappear. The Nicene Creed rejected this obviously false and unbiblical doctrine by stating that Jesus Christ, the Son of God, would rule forever in his future kingdom. He wasn't destined to be reabsorbed back into God's amorphous divinity.

The most significant expansion between the creeds of 325 and 381 occurred in the third article. The original creed had simply said, "We believe in the Holy Spirit." But since that time, the Spirit Fighters had come on the scene, and the Three Cappadocians had engaged them with a theological counteroffensive. As we saw earlier, these three churchmen had slightly different views about the proper terminology for the Spirit. Basil of Caesarea was reluctant to call him "God," while Gregory of Nyssa affirmed his total unity with the Father and Son. Gregory of Nazianzus wanted to go the whole way and use the term "God" for all three Trinitarian persons. Unfortunately, though the latter Gregory was briefly the council chair, he left early due to church politics. Gregory wasn't there at the end to insist on the full equivalence of the Father, Son, and Holy Spirit in clear terms.

Therefore, the final clause of the Nicene Creed left its pneumatology a little bit vague. No question, the Spirit is divine, for he is "worshiped and glorified" with the other two persons. The Holy Spirit is he who inspired the Old Testament prophets (Num. 24:2; 1 Sam. 10:10; 2 Sam. 23:2; Isa. 61:1) and gives life to humankind (John 6:63; Rom. 8:11).

The Holy Spirit can even be called "Lord"—the same term used of Yahweh in the Old Testament and of Jesus in the New.

Nevertheless, the Nicene Creed didn't come out and say that *homoousios* applies to the Spirit like it does to the other two persons of the Trinity. The theologians of the day were trying to find a delicate balance among various viewpoints. Modern historian Sara Parvis provides us a wise reminder when she remarks, "One is often tempted—I am myself—to see Constantinople 381 as the weakest of the early ecumenical councils, and be frustrated that it did not promulgate a clearer theology of the consubstantiality of the Holy Spirit with the other two persons of the Trinity. But sometimes theological strength is best seen in weakness—and Constantinople 381 might well be one of those times."[8]

A final important change to the pneumatological third article of the Nicene Creed was its inclusion of some assertions about the church and the end times. Although these didn't appear in the statement of 325, perhaps they should have, for they were common aspects of early Christian baptismal creeds, especially from the second century on. Typically, such statements would appear in the third article of creeds because the Holy Spirit is the person of the Trinity who indwells the church.

Modern people only have to think of the Apostles' Creed for a parallel. It states, "I believe in the Holy Spirit, the holy catholic church, the communion of saints, the forgiveness of sins, the resurrection of the body, and the life everlasting. Amen." The similarities between this formula and the Nicene Creed can easily be discerned. When the council members of 381 added such pronouncements, they weren't innovating, just bringing their new version into conformity with the creeds they had long been using in their pastoral oversight of Christian baptism.

Victory Achieved—Now What?

The Council of Constantinople adjourned in July 381 with its primary objective accomplished: to confirm and reestablish the creed of 325—and thus Nicene Trinitarianism—as the official faith of the Christian church. The delegates didn't see themselves as having written a replacement creed. Theirs was merely a slightly adapted version that made plain what the original one at Nicaea had intended. The bishops dispersed from Constantinople and went home with the awareness that a great victory had been achieved. Unity had prevailed over doctrinal squabbles. No doubt, Emperor Theodosius breathed a sigh of relief.

But what happened next? Was Arianism immediately stamped out? How did its now-discredited adherents respond? How did the Nicene Creed work its way so deeply into church life that it became the one statement that could unite all types of Christians? Did anyone ever attempt to change this definitive creed? If so, what happened to them? What is the status of the Nicene Creed today? Questions like these will occupy our next chapter before we finally turn our thoughts to some lessons about the essential meaning of Nicene Trinitarianism.

Part 4

The Legacy of Nicaea

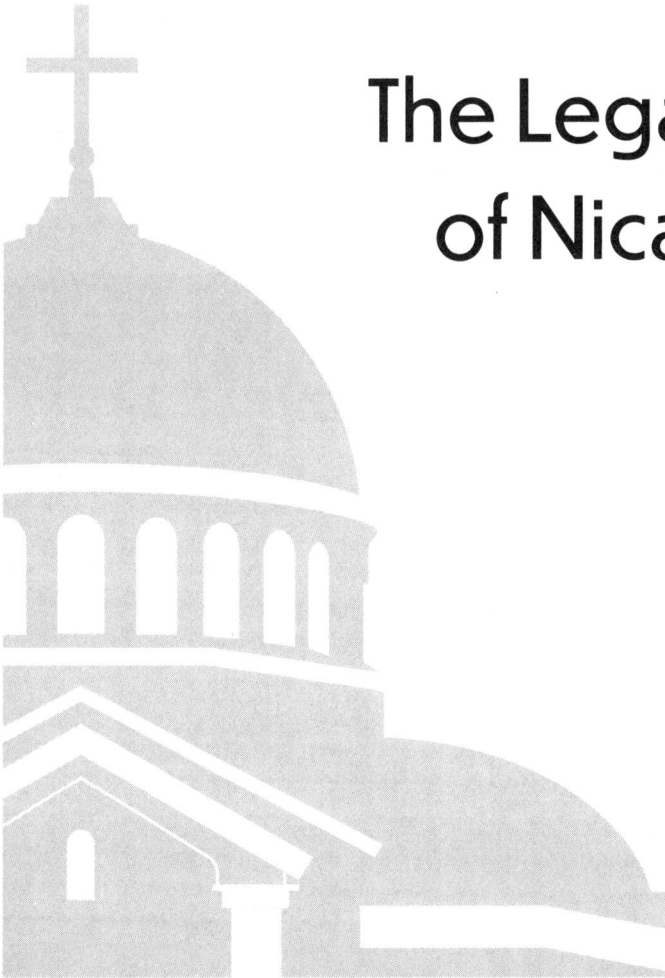

13

Later History of the Nicene Creed

For a few decades in the middle of the fourth century, it looked like Nicene Trinitarianism was going to succumb to some type of Arian theology. Though exactly which view would prevail couldn't yet be determined, the one set forth at Nicaea in 325 seemed likely to fizzle and be lost in the sands of time. Whether Christ would be called "similar," "similar in essence," or even "dissimilar" to the Father wasn't clear. But in the end, it wouldn't matter. If the consubstantiality of the Trinity came to be denied, all would be lost. At least, that was how Athanasius saw things—and that's why he fought so hard for Nicaea's creed, even if it meant standing *contra mundum*, "against the world."

Yet as time went on, none of the Arian theologies prevailed. After Theodosius came to power and called his council in 381, Nicene Christianity experienced a renaissance. Since then, all orthodox believers have confessed the full and eternal deity of the Father, Son, and Holy Spirit. That is a

159

very good thing. A lesser Christ—a Christ who is inferior to the Father's divinity in any way—would undercut the essence of the Christian gospel.

Of course, when the Council of Constantinople ended, the various Arian factions didn't disappear overnight. Where did they go after Theodosius excluded them from the true faith? Did the Arians just slink away without a fight? Of course not. So what was their future trajectory? And how did the Nicene Creed's own trajectory rocket through the ages into the present day?

The Fate of the Arians

The most powerful Arian bishop during the early fourth century wasn't Arius himself, but Eusebius of Nicomedia, the theological and pastoral confidant of Emperor Constantine. When Constantine approached his death in 337, it was Eusebius whom he invited to preside over his baptism. Eusebius died only four years later, in 341. Just before the powerful bishop went to meet his Maker, he did something that would have far-reaching consequences. He ordained a young man named Ulfilas as a missionary to the "barbarians."

Politically speaking, the era after Constantine was Rome's last gasp. At this time, Germanic peoples were invading, immigrating, and integrating into imperial lands. Quite often, these notably tall and strong men joined the Roman army, which was happy to take them as mercenaries when regular troops were scarce. One of the main Germanic tribes was the Goths. They weren't actually savage and crude "barbarians"—that is an unfair term that the Romans imposed on them. They were just a different people group from regions north of the Rhine and Danube rivers, which lay outside the empire.

Ulfilas was the son of Roman parents who had been trafficked into the borderlands after a Gothic raid. He was raised as a Christian among the pagan Goths. In young adulthood, he was sent back into the empire as an ambassador. There he learned about Arian doctrine, which he quickly embraced. That was why Eusebius of Nicomedia ordained him as a missionary bishop. Ulfilas returned to the Goths and oversaw the development of a new script for their language, which allowed the Bible to be translated into that tongue for the first time. The missionary work met with resounding success. The Goths became devoted Arians, believing in Jesus but not his consubstantiality with the Father. Other Germanic tribes soon followed. The "barbarians" had begun to be Christianized, though they didn't yet have good, accurate theology.

Ulfilas had a disciple named Auxentius, whose confrontation with the great Bishop Ambrose of Milan has come to be called the "Affair of the Basilicas." It was a dramatic moment when Arianism and Nicene Trinitarianism met head-on. What happened?

A young teenager, Valentinian II, ruled as emperor over Italy in 385. Due to his youth, his mother, Empress Justina, actually held the reins of power. Since she favored Arianism, she ordered Ambrose—a staunch Nicene believer—to hand over a Milanese church so the Arians could celebrate Easter rites in it. Ambrose flatly refused, leading to a stalemate.

But the following Easter, in 386, the controversy resurfaced—and this time, Empress Justina was prepared to back up her demands with legal maneuvers and Gothic troops. Through her son, she passed a law that claimed all Arians had a right to worship in Italy, where the decrees of Theodosius hadn't yet taken effect. When the imperial court in

Mosaic of Ambrose in the church of St. Ambrogio of Milan.

161

Atrium of the Basilica of Saint Ambrose. Photo by Óðinn
(Wikimedia Commons, CC BY-SA 2.5).

Milan demanded that the Christian basilica be handed over
to Auxentius for impious worship, Ambrose and his congregation set up camp in it and refused to leave.

On Palm Sunday, Ambrose delivered a sermon while his
church was surrounded by soldiers. "Were you afraid that
I should desert the church and forsake you in fear for my
own safety?" he asked his worried congregants. Certainly
not! Ambrose promised that "to desert the church had never
entered my mind; for I feared the Lord of the universe more
than an earthly emperor."[1] Of course, he would gladly go
and debate theology at the emperor's palace if he could be
certain the basilica wouldn't be "given over to heretics." Yet
Ambrose knew that as soon as he departed the building, the
troops would rush in. Instead, the brave bishop confronted
the emperor with ringing words that would set the pattern
for church-state struggles in western Europe for the next

1,400 years: "The emperor is in the church," Ambrose declared, "not above it."[2]

In the end, Valentinian II and his mother were forced to back down. A great victory had been won for the freedom of the catholic church, as well as for the Nicene doctrine that it now embraced. From this point on, Christians everywhere held to the doctrine of the Trinity, led especially by the bishops of Rome in the West and Constantinople in the East. Though the Arian heresy continued to be held among the Germanic tribes, over the next few centuries it gradually faded as each of these people groups morphed into the Christian kingdoms of early medieval Europe. One by one, they decided that they, too, wanted to hold the Nicene faith like the bishop of Rome.

Interestingly, though, the shape of Nicene belief in western Europe took a noteworthy turn in the Middle Ages. The Latin world introduced a theological change with which the Easterners disagreed. The change at first seemed subtle—a minor point about the Holy Spirit. Yet, in the end, it helped to break Christendom wide open and create two global denominations of the Christian faith.

The Double Procession of the Spirit

As we learned in chapter 1 of this book, the purpose of creeds is to confess them aloud; that is, to "same say" the words that other believers hold as well. Unity arises when everyone agrees on the same verbal statement, even if it varies slightly according to the translation being used.

In the case of today's Nicene Creed, all Christians recite essentially the same words—except in one clause. The third article in the rewritten creed of 381 had declared that the Holy Spirit "proceeds from the Father." Greek Orthodox Christians still say it that way. But Westerners—Roman

Catholics and Protestants, including evangelicals—add the phrase, "and from the Son." This is called the "double procession" of the Spirit. How did this discrepancy arise in the Nicene Creed? And more importantly, is it correct?

To reach a good answer, we need to understand a general principle about the Trinitarianism that developed in the Latin-speaking West versus the Greek-speaking East. During the ancient church period, these two regions set distinct theological trajectories that are still part of Roman Catholicism and Protestantism (or "Western" theology) and Greek Orthodoxy (or "Eastern" theology).

Broadly speaking, Western Trinitarianism has emphasized the oneness of God: the total unity of the Trinity. When taken to the extreme, this can lead to modalism, which collapses the three persons into a single God who only has different "modes" of self-expression. In that case, unity is being preserved at the expense of interpersonal diversity. But as long as the error of modalism is avoided, the oneness of God is an important theological principle.

Yet so his threeness. The Greek East has always insisted that the Trinitarian persons are just that: three distinct persons who have dynamic, interactive relationships with each other. They are not abstract forces or principles within the Godhead. The theological temptation here, of course, is to separate the persons so much that the Second and Third become alienated from the substance of the First—and thus become inferior to him. These were precisely the errors of the Arians and the Spirit Fighters. If these inaccuracies can be avoided, however, the interpersonal threeness of God is a vital truth. Nicene Trinitarianism tries to safeguard both sides of the divine mystery: relational diversity combined with monotheistic unity for all eternity.

The problem with the Nicene Creed's expression that the Spirit "proceeds from the Father" is that the Son appears to be uninvolved. To an Eastern theologian, that could perhaps be acceptable. Procession is simply an aspect of the relationship between the First and Third Persons. But for Westerners, that would undercut the unity of the Trinity by making the Second Person seem like an irrelevant bystander. This could lead to the Son being inferior within the Trinity, as Arianism would teach. The Western church had long claimed that the Spirit came from the Father *through* the Son. Tertullian had said this in the early third century, and Ambrose said it in the late fourth.[3] In fact, some Eastern fathers said it as well.[4] Nevertheless, the concept of double procession didn't make it into the Nicene Creed of 381, at least not explicitly.

The key Bible verse is John 15:26, where Jesus declares, "But when the Helper comes, whom I will send to you from the Father, the Spirit of truth, who *proceeds from the Father*, he will bear witness about me" (italics mine).[5] The phrase "proceeds from the Father" in the Nicene Creed uses the same Greek verb as the one used by John. Procession from the Father seems pretty clear in this verse. Yet notice that Jesus said he will send the Spirit from the Father. The Western church read that part and exclaimed, "See? The Son wasn't uninvolved! The Holy Spirit proceeds from him too!"

The greatest theologian of the ancient church—and certainly one of the greatest of all time—was Augustine of Hippo. He believed in the doctrines of Nicaea. In fact, his own mother, Monica, had stood with Bishop Ambrose in the besieged

Augustine of Hippo by Sandro Botticelli, ca. 1490.

basilica, singing hymns with her pastor as they defended their church against Empress Justina and the Arians. Yet Augustine's profound work, *On the Trinity*, did much more than engage with the Nicene-Arian controversy. Augustine broke new theological ground as he considered the tri-unity of God. In so doing, he launched the Western medieval trajectory of double procession.

The brilliant bishop of Hippo emphasized that the Holy Spirit is especially (though not exclusively) identified with the biblical concepts of "gift" and "love."[6] The Father loves the Son, and the Son returns that love. But in eternity past, "love" couldn't have been something separate and self-existent that the Father and Son participated in. Nothing existed before the world's creation except the Trinity. So where was love to be found in the distant past? The Spirit must have been the bond of love that the other two persons shared between them.

Of course, a love so rich and beautiful couldn't be kept to itself. That is why God shared it with humanity as a gift. According to the apostle Paul, "God's *love* has been poured into our hearts through the Holy Spirit who has been *given* to us" (Rom. 5:5, italics mine). Likewise, the apostle John said, "God is *love*," and "By this we know that we abide in him and he in us, because he has *given* us of his Spirit" (1 John 4:8, 13, italics mine). The Spirit of love is the bountiful gift of God to the human race. Augustine couldn't fathom a view of the Trinity in which the Father would give a gift apart from the Son. Instead, they jointly bestowed upon humanity the Holy Spirit who personifies their own vibrant, living love.

Over time, Augustine's theology percolated throughout the Latin-speaking world. Beginning in Spain in the 500s, then spreading throughout medieval Europe in the time of Charlemagne (800s), double procession came to be an essential Trinitarian doctrine. The Latin translation of the Nicene

Creed had originally said the Spirit proceeds *ex Patre*, "from the Father." Now the medieval European church added to the text of the creed the phrase *filioque* (pronounced "fil-ee-OH-kway"). This addition declared that the Spirit proceeds from the Father "and from the Son."

The so-called *filioque* clause became a point of sharp contention between the Latin and Greek churches. The Westerners said popes could amend the creed if necessary, whereas the Easterners said the authority of creeds stood above all bishops, even the one in Rome. Eventually, this dispute contributed to a formal split into two separate denominations. The Roman Catholic and Eastern Orthodox churches divided from each other in 1054 during what is known as the Great Schism. The two churches went their separate ways, each confessing the Nicene Creed with the wording they saw fit.

When the Reformation came along in the 1500s, none of the Protestants disagreed with the Catholics about the *filioque* clause. Their debates were about entirely different issues. Therefore, modern Protestants still include "and from the Son" when they recite the Nicene Creed. Perhaps such recitation doesn't happen often in Protestant churches, but whenever it does, the additional phrase is included. And this raises the final topic for our chapter: What are the historical precedents for Protestants reciting this ancient creed in modern times?

Confessing the Creed

Let's take a look at the big picture. Who, today, recites the Nicene Creed? Certainly, the Greek Orthodox do. As soon as it was read into the record at the Council of Chalcedon in 451, it began to be used annually as part of the church's catechesis prior to baptism on Easter morning. In the late

400s, it was introduced into the weekly eucharistic service at Antioch. Then in 511, the bishop of Constantinople, Timothy I, mandated public recitation of the Nicene Creed as part of the standard Greek liturgy. The practice spread widely across the Greek-speaking world. Ever since then, the Nicene Creed has been, and still is, confessed every single Sunday in Eastern Orthodox churches around the globe.

Likewise, Roman Catholic churches have used it through many centuries. As in the East, so in the West; the creed was incorporated into baptismal instruction starting in the 500s. Not long after this, it entered the Spanish liturgy of the weekly Sunday service—with its *filioque* addition, of course—in order to counter the Gothic Arianism that still existed there. Then the Nicene Creed jumped over to Ireland, a land that had many sea trading contacts with Spain. From Ireland, its weekly usage spread to Britain, and from Britain, it entered the Frankish empire of Charlemagne. At last, around 1014, the pope of Rome also accepted it into the regular eucharistic liturgy in Italy. From that date forward, the standard service of the Catholic Mass has included recitation of the Nicene Creed. It is located after the Scripture readings and sermon, and just prior to communion, or Holy Eucharist.

But what about Protestants? There are four main branches of the Reformation, and three of them have formally accepted the Nicene Creed as sound doctrine. It can be profitably recited as part of the Sunday service. These Protestant affirmations go back to the 1500s and have not been rescinded. The Lutheran tradition incorporates the Nicene Creed in its *Book of Concord*, along with the Apostles' and Athanasian creeds.[7] The Reformed (Calvinistic/Presbyterian) tradition states in the Belgic Confession, Article 9, that "we willingly accept the three ecumenical creeds—the Apostles', Nicene, and Athanasian—as well as what the ancient fathers decided in agreement with them."[8] And the *Book of Common Prayer* from the Anglican tradition (the Church of England or Episcopal Church) inserts the creed into the weekly liturgy at the same place as the Catholics: after the Scripture readings and sermon and before Holy Eucharist.[9]

The fourth branch, however, tends to put less stock in creeds. The Free Church (Anabaptist) tradition has typically been the least likely of the four Reformation strands to accept formal creeds, even long-standing ones like the Nicene. Modern churches with deep roots in this tradition include Baptists and "Bible church" or nondenominational evangelicals. Among these groups, the slogan "No creed but the Bible!" is often heard. Reading a creed aloud is rare in such churches. If one is recited, it would tend to be the Apostles' Creed more often than the Nicene.

But why should this be? Though the Apostles' Creed is a very good statement, full of rich theology, the Nicene Creed is even more ancient and widely attested. Furthermore, the Nicene Creed is Christianity's most specific and concise explanation of the Trinity. As we will see in our final chapter, the Trinity isn't just a metaphysical abstraction or a quirk of church history. It is a fundamental description of the God who saves. To confess the Nicene view of the Trinity is to proclaim the Christian gospel.

14

The Trinity as the Gospel

You don't have to hang around the Christian world for very long before you hear the word "gospel." Sometimes it's used as a noun: the message of eternal salvation. More recently, it has become a popular adjective that gets attached to other words: gospel living, gospel mission, gospel ministry, gospel people, gospel churches. And on it goes. Everyone assumes we know what the word "gospel" means, that we all have a shared concept of it. But do we really? And if we do, is it accurate?

At its core, we tend to think of the gospel as a spiritual thing. It belongs in the realm of churches and religion. Every pastor talks about it. Every congregation wants to embody it. Every Christian blogger defines it. Every missionary proclaims it. The gospel is at the heart of Christianity. Surely, this is a biblical word, right?

Yes, it is.

But before it was Christian, the word had a life of its own.

The Greek word *euangelion*—latinized as *evangelium*, anglicized as the "evangel"—has its conceptual roots not in the religious sphere but in war and conquest. Long before Jesus Christ walked this earth, Greek and Roman people were proclaiming the gospel of victory. Literally, this word combines the prefix for "good" (*eu-*) with the word for a "message" or "announcement" (*angelia*). It means "good news," or specifically, the public proclamation of a king's victory after a battle and the establishment of his new kingdom to replace the defeated one.

Did you know that one of the world's first evangelists wasn't a Christian but the great Roman emperor Caesar Augustus? At the end of his life, he erected an inscription across the empire (basically, he commissioned billboard advertisements everywhere), which touted his many achievements. This massive propaganda piece, totaling four thousand words in English translation, was known as the *Res Gestae*, which means "things accomplished." A gospel message was a verbal proclamation of mighty deeds. In fact, another famous inscription

The Temple of Augustus and Rome in Ankara, Turkey, with the Res Gestae Divi Augusti ("Deeds of the Divine Augustus") inscribed on the walls of the cella. Photo by Carole Raddato (Wikimedia Commons, CC BY-SA 2.0).

from 9 BC says, "the birthday of the god Augustus was the beginning of the good news [*euangelion*] for the world."

All of this serves as the background to the Christian appropriation of the word "gospel." The early church triumphed over Rome not by introducing the idea of a gospel, but by switching which gospel was being preached. Like the emperors, the first believers also had a declaration of good news. Of course, theirs wasn't a gospel of domination and glory by the edge of a sword. That was Rome's message. Yet the Christian counter-message might not be what you think it was. The gospel wasn't a description of personal salvation, a means by which individual people could "get saved" by their decision of faith. The gospel of the early church didn't start with a personal problem and provide a strategy for its solution.

Rather, like any gospel announcement in the ancient world, it started with a proclamation of royal victory over a defeated regime. And right along with that proclamation—inherent within it, in fact—was a demand for all hearers to offer willing subjection to the new king. Those who resist the Victor will find his message to be bad news. However, those who embrace him will hear good tidings and begin to flourish. Only then will their sins be forgiven by grace. Only then will they begin to be saved, enduring to the end to gain a share of the Victor's crown. But the present decision that the hearer must make isn't the primary substance of the gospel. Nor are its future ramifications. What comes first in a true gospel proclamation is an announcement of a finished work in the past: the "things accomplished" by the Lord who has won the battle.

God Became Man

The victory of Jesus on that first Easter morning forms the climax of the gospel. All of his victories that still lie ahead—the blessed day when Satan will be cast into the abyss, when death will no longer reign, when sin and suffering will be no more—all of these find their source in the fact of the empty tomb. Although Rome crucified the Savior of the world with its worst form of capital punishment, although his body was broken on the tree and the religious leaders spat in his face—even so, that wasn't the last word. Instead, as the angel proclaimed at sunrise, "He is risen" (Matt. 28:6 NLT). And all God's people replied, "He is risen indeed!" This is good news beyond compare.

But if all of that lies *ahead* in the story's resolution, where does the gospel story *begin*? We cannot—we dare not!—start the story with the crucifixion. A popular saying, derived from C. S. Lewis's book *The Weight of Glory*, claims that "the cross comes before the crown."[1] In other words, only after Jesus's crucifixion can glory be achieved. Fair enough; there is some truth to that.

Yet, at the most basic level, the Christological story doesn't begin with the cross. It begins with the crib, the animal manger in which the helpless Lord Jesus was laid, dirty, dependent, and disregarded. In other words, the fundamental truth of the gospel isn't "Jesus died on the cross" but "God became man." All else flows from the incarnation: the obedient life of Christ; his death, burial, descent, resurrection, ascension, and session at the Father's right hand; and his imminent return for judgments and rewards. This cosmic narrative testifies to what humankind truly is: the object of God's inevitable, redeeming love. Human beings are so important to God that his Son became one of them for the sake of their salvation.

And this is precisely where Trinitarianism intersects with the gospel, where they are revealed not to be separate truths but intertwined ones. The council fathers at Nicaea believed that Jesus was born of a virgin, lived a holy life, died on the cross, and rose from the dead. But so did the Arians! The point that truly mattered was: *Who* was that unborn child in the uterus of a Hebrew girl? *Who* writhed in agony on a Roman cross? *Who* exited the garden tomb? *Who* sits at the Father's right hand? *Who* is coming again to judge the living and dead?

Nicene Trinitarianism answered those questions in a fundamentally different way from the Arians. The heretics said a lesser being had come down. But the Nicene Creed insisted that he who came down "for us and for our salvation" was in every way the LORD God. Jesus Christ is Yahweh in the flesh. He is the Most High, Adonai, El Shaddai. He is the Ancient of Days, the Everlasting Father, the Prince of Peace. No mere messenger. No inferior being. No creature formed at a moment before which "he was not." None of that! The Son who is fully God—*homoousios* with the Father—is the one who lay smeared with afterbirth in a wooden manger, then lay bloodied once more upon a cold, stone slab. Let this astonishing truth make you marvel: God . . . became . . . man. That is the gospel of the Christian faith!

Delighting in the Trinity

If the Trinity reveals that God became a human being, what does that mean for us? What are the ramifications of such an awesome and dazzling truth? I would like to close this book by suggesting a twofold application. First, the doctrine of the Trinity tells us something essential about the character of God: that he not only knows how to love, or practices love, or celebrates love, but that *he is love itself.* Every good and beautiful thing that we mean by the word "love" finds its source in God. Whatever love is, that is precisely what God is.

Second, the Trinity tells us something about ourselves: We humans are beloved by God on a colossal scale, to a degree that is nearly incomprehensible. When God became a human being, the Word became flesh. The incarnation of Jesus is a heavenly message written not with ink but with blood. A Bible may come to us on paper, but even better is the Word of God that comes in skin and bones. When that message hits us, it hits us hard because it hits us fully enfleshed. Human beings are so beloved by God that he would dare to join us in our sorrowful state of affliction. It was inevitably, invariably, indubitably the case that God intended to become one of us. Yahweh is on our side like no other god in the pantheons of human-made religion. He is *Deus pro nobis*—God for us. And if that One is for us, who can be against us?

One of the best modern studies of Trinitarianism comes from the English theologian Michael Reeves in his popular book, *Delighting in the Trinity*. In one of his chapters, Reeves asks, "What was God doing before creation?" The answer is found in John 17:24, where Jesus declares to his Father, "You loved me before the foundation of the world." The eternally generated Son has always been the recipient of the Father's life-giving love. Therefore, the Son delights to return that love. And as they love each other, the Spirit enlivens the dynamic between them, so he is loved by each as well.

If there were no such thing as the Trinity, God could not *be* love. A solitary God could *begin* to love once he had made something to receive his affection. But before there was anything else, if God were alone, he would have no one to love but himself, and that is the very definition of narcissism. Even a dual God could not show love except in an exclusive, ungenerous kind of way, like an infatuated couple whose obsession turns them both inward. But with three, the relationship becomes communal. Such love can be bountiful, turned outward toward the other, and marked by a willingness to share. "When the love between two persons is happy, healthy, and secure, they rejoice to share it," Reeves remarks. "Just so it is with God."[2] The Trinity is a community of generous felicity.

But there's more. Because divine love is so infinite and free, it doesn't stay contained within the trifold relationship of the Godhead. It overflows into creation because life-making and love-sharing are so inherent to the Trinity. God creates a universe, not out of compulsion, but because the generous dynamic of the three persons deserves to be lived out in a cosmos by image-bearers. "So why did God create?" Reeves asks. "Because God delights to spread His goodness. In other words, He is like a sun of goodness, blazing out with love. . . . He created because He was so happily bursting with goodness. God is so overflowingly, super-abundantly full of life in Himself that He delighted to spread His goodness. His innermost being is a sun of light, life and warmth, always shining *out*: radiant and outgoing."[3]

God becoming man tells us all we need to know about humanity—and at the same time, it sets before our eyes a mystery that we'll spend eternity trying to grasp. If God had sent a mere demigod to us, we might have been suitably impressed. A second-tier deity would still be quite a messenger. But that isn't what happened—not at all! The Nicene Creed declares that the God who loves us sent God to become one of us so God could indwell us. Each divine person has a role to play. Only a Trinity can do such a marvelous thing.

The eternal relationship in heaven doesn't stand closed off from us. We humans—sinners, every one of us—are invited to enter the triune dynamic. Jesus says to his Father about his followers, "The glory that you have given me I have given to them, that they may be one even as we are one" (John 17:22). Notice what Jesus is saying. The Father has given the riches of divine glory to his Son, but Jesus refuses to hoard it for himself. Instead, he shares it with us, so that by grace we might partake of what the Trinity possesses by nature.

The consubstantiality of the three persons—the way that they are "one"—can be ours as well. Believers in Jesus are consubstantial with each other through the indwelling Spirit. We possess the same unity that marks the triune God. The kind of love that would offer such bounty is generous beyond comprehension.

The twentieth-century Swiss theologian Karl Barth understood these truths and expressed them often. In his era, the advocates of liberal theology had relegated the Trinity to a foolish, insignificant footnote in the history of doctrine. Barth almost singlehandedly recovered the centrality of Trinitarian dogmatics, giving them back to mainstream theology like living water rushing onto barren ground. More than anyone else in his generation—or perhaps ever!—Barth recognized the profundity of the statement, "God became man." Such an infinite condescension sends a message. When the one who is fully God unites himself to fallen human flesh, it declares the truth that *Deus pro nobis*: God is for us. He is on our side, willing to join us in our oppression so we might be elevated back to the Creator from whom we had fallen away.

I can think of no better way to end this book than with a quotation from Barth's essay *The Humanity of God*, which comes from lectures he delivered in 1956. As you read these words, I ask you to recognize that they place a demand upon you. Divine love of such magnitude calls for a response—not just generally from humanity, but *your own* response. The Trinity has always existed as love. But once you become aware of how deeply that love is directed toward *you*, what will your response be? Will you enter (perhaps for the first time? perhaps now more deeply?) into the life of the risen Christ, and thus be caught up in the Trinitarian dynamic of love's reception, return, and overflow to others? Or will you continue to miss out on what the consubstantial Father, Son, and Holy Spirit have to offer you? Consider your decision as you read the profound words of Professor Barth. He says:

> We do not need to engage in a free-ranging investigation to seek out and construct who and what God truly is, and who and what man truly is, but only to read the truth about both where it resides, namely, in the fullness of their togetherness, their covenant which proclaims itself in Jesus Christ. . . .
>
> God's deity is thus no prison in which he can exist only in and for himself. It is rather his freedom to be in and for himself but also with and for us, to assert but also to sacrifice himself, to be wholly exalted but also completely humble, not only almighty but also almighty mercy, not only Lord but also servant, not only judge but also himself the judged, not only man's eternal king but also his brother in time. And all that without in the slightest forfeiting his deity! All that, rather, in the highest proof and proclamation of his deity! . . .
>
> It would be the false deity of a false God if in his deity his humanity did not also immediately encounter us. Such false deities are by Jesus Christ once for all made a laughingstock. In him the fact is once for all established that God does not exist without man.[4]

"God does not exist without man." Amen! He exists for the sake of humanity. And indeed, Nicene Trinitarianism reveals that God even exists *as* a human being. The only question, then, is: Will humans continue to live without God?

Notes

Chapter 1 What Is a Creed?

1. "Original Wisconsin Ducks," Wisconsin Dells, accessed July 1, 2024, https://www.wisdells.com/wisconsin-dells-attractions/Original -Wisconsin-Ducks.

Chapter 2 Out of Nature, Many Gods

1. Pascal Boyer, *Religion Explained: The Evolutionary Origins of Religious Thought* (Basic Books, 2001).
2. Justin L. Barrett, *Why Would Anyone Believe in God?* (AltaMira Press, 2004).

Chapter 3 Out of Many Gods, One Lord

1. Jaroslav Pelikan and Valerie Hotchkiss, *Creeds and Confessions of Faith in the Christian Tradition* (Yale, 2003), 1:29.

Chapter 4 Does Yahweh Have a Son?

1. Plato, *Timaeus*, trans. Donald J. Zeyl (Hackett Publishing Company, 2000), 14.
2. Philo, *On Dreams* 1.215.
3. *Wisdom of Solomon* 2:13, 16, 18; 5:5.

Chapter 5 Jesus the Son of God

1. Sir Lancelot C. L. Brenton, *The Septuagint LXX: Greek and English* (Samuel Bagster & Sons, 1851), https://ccel.org/bible/brenton/index.html.

Chapter 6 Maybe Jesus *Is* the Father?

1. Ernest Evans, *Tertullian's Treatise Against Praxeas: The Text Edited, with an Introduction, Translation, and Commentary* 13.4 (SPCK, 1948), 31–38.

2. Evans, *Tertullian* 15.1, 151.

3. Evans, *Tertullian* 12.7, 146.

Chapter 7 Always a Father, Always a Son

1. Henry Wadsworth Longfellow, "There Was a Little Girl," quoted in *The World's Best Poetry*, ed. Bliss Carman (The University Society, Inc., 1904), 1:169.

2. Irenaeus of Lyons, *Against Heresies* 4.20.1, 5.6.1.

3. Other verses that depict Christ as the instrument of God's creative work include John 1:3, John 1:10, and Colossians 1:16–17.

4. The Bible of the early church fathers didn't yet have chapters or verses, but the references are supplied to help modern readers identify which Scriptures are under discussion.

5. Sir Lancelot C. L. Brenton, *The Septuagint LXX: Greek and English* (Samuel Bagster & Sons, 1851), https://ccel.org/bible/brenton/index.html.

6. Origen, *On First Principles* 1.2.4, in *Origen: On First Principles*, trans. G. W. Butterworth (Peter Smith, 1973), 17–18.

Chapter 8 The Rise of Heresy

1. Socrates Scholasticus, *Church History* 1.5, in *Nicene and Post-Nicene Fathers*, series 2 (NPNF2), ed. Philip Schaff and Henry Wace (Hendrickson, 1995), 2:3. I have slightly edited the outdated translations of the NPNF texts throughout this book for better clarity.

2. An ancient church historian named Philostorgius wrote an account of these matters, but it hasn't survived. Fortunately, a medieval writer named Photius owned a copy, and he made a summary of what he read. He recorded that Arius "wrote songs for sailing, grinding [grain], traveling, and so on, set them to music he thought suitable to each, and through the pleasure given by the music [he] stole away the simpler folk for his own heresy." Photius, *Epitome* 2.2, in *Philostorgius: Church History*, trans. Philip R. Amidon (SBL, 2007), 16; The Christian bishop Athanasius also complained about Arius's doctrinal songs, particularly one titled "The Banquet," which contained the slogan "There was when the Son was not" and many other Arian ideas. Athanasius said such tunes were enjoyed by bawdy men "who sing such strains over their cups, amid cheers and jokes, when men are merry, that the rest may laugh." Arius's poetic style for these songs imitated the Greek poet named Sotades who was famous

for his obscene lyrics. Athanasius, *Oration Against the Arians* 1.4, in *NPNF2*, ed. Philip Schaff and Henry Wace (Hendrickson, 1892), 4:308.

3. This word has nothing to do with the white supremacist or Nazi term "Aryan."

4. A similar view is held today by Mormons and Jehovah's Witnesses.

5. Rufinus, *Church History* 10.1, in *Rufinus of Aquileia: History of the Church*, trans. Philip R. Amidon (Catholic University of America, 2016), 380.

6. Scholasticus, *Church History* 1.6, in *NPNF2* 2:3, 5.

Chapter 9 Constantine's Council

1. A few years later, when Licinius started making trouble again, Constantine quietly dispatched his exiled rival into the afterlife.

2. This symbol is called the Christogram. It took the form of either a Chi-Rho (☧) or a Tau-Rho (⳨), though the former is more commonly associated with Constantine today. Chi and rho are the first two Greek letters of the word "Christ," while tau and rho are part of the Greek word for "cross" and "crucifixion." This second ligature also looks like a small graphic of a crucified man. Both were preexisting Christian symbols used as scribal abbreviations in biblical manuscripts when those words appeared in the text. Emperor Constantine adopted them as his own and made them famous in church history, especially the Chi-Rho.

3. My own view is that the conversion was a genuine, early turn to Jesus, yet it took several years to lose its pagan syncretism and become authentically Christian. I have imagined what that process might have looked like in my three novels in the Constantine's Empire trilogy: *The Conqueror*, *Every Knee Shall Bow*, and *Caesar's Lord* (Revell, 2020, 2021, 2022).

4. Constantine is to be commended for his well-worded, conciliatory letter that seeks Christian unity and peace. Unfortunately, his approach was—to borrow a phrase from Teddy Roosevelt—"peace at any price." The emperor dismissed as insignificant some issues that actually addressed the fundamental nature of Jesus, and thus affected the heart of the gospel. Later, Constantine learned to treat these issues with the importance they are due. "Letter of Emperor Constantine to Alexander of Alexandria and Arius," Fourth Century Christianity, updated January 1, 2025, https://www.fourthcentury.com/urkunde-17/.

5. "Letter of Emperor Constantine," Fourth Century Christianity.

6. The council's full decree can be read at https://www.fourthcentury.com/urkunde-18/.

7. The traditional number of attendees mentioned often in church history is 318. Probably, this was a legendary reference to the number of Abraham's servants in Genesis 14:14.

8. Eusebius of Caesarea, *Life of Constantine* 3.10, in *Eusebius: Life of Constantine*, trans. Averil Cameron and Stuart G. Hall (Clarendon, 1999), 125.

9. Theodoret of Cyrus, *Ecclesiastical History* 1.6., *NPNF2*, ed. Philip Schaff and Henry Wace (Hendrickson, 1892), 3:43.

10. There is no ancient church evidence for the popular notion, often seen today on the web or on social media, that Nicholas of Myra slapped Arius at the Nicene council for his blasphemies. The modern joke now includes the pun that Santa cried, "Ho! Ho! *Homoousios!*" Though this is certainly amusing, the events probably didn't occur. The first time such a thing is mentioned is 1370 (notice: more than a thousand years after the fact), when a biographer of the saint said that Nicholas slapped "an Arian." By the late 1500s, the legend had been clarified to designate a slap of Arius himself. Today, the image of Nicholas slapping Arius is an acceptable aspect of what may be depicted in Greek Orthodox icons.

11. Eusebius, *Life of Constantine* 3.15, 127.

Chapter 10 The Debate Rages On, Part 1

1. Sara Parvis, "The Reception of Nicaea and *Homoousios* to 360," in *The Cambridge Companion to the Council of Nicaea*, ed. Young Richard Kim (Cambridge, 2021), 225.

2. Athanasius, *Letter 54, To Serapion*, in *NPNF2*, ed. Philip Schaff and Henry Wace (Hendrickson, 1892), 4:565. See also Socrates Scholasticus, *Church History* 1.38, in *NPNF2*, ed. Philip Schaff and Henry Wace (Hendrickson, 1995), 2:35.

3. Adapted from Rufinus, *Church History* 10.15, in *Rufinus of Aquileia: History of the Church*, trans. Philip Amidon (Catholic University of America, 2016), 405–6.

4. Jerome, *Dialogue Against Luciferians* 19, in *NPNF2*, ed. Philip Schaff and Henry Wace (Hendrickson, 1893), 6:329.

5. Parvis, "Reception," 229.

6. The phrase *Athanasius contra mundum* was used by the evangelist and founder of Methodism, John Wesley, in a letter to antislavery crusader William Wilberforce. Wesley exhorted Wilberforce to stand firm against slavery with the same resolve as Athanasius. See Albert C. Outler, ed., *John Wesley* (Oxford University Press, 1980), 85–86. Wesley appears to be quoting the earlier description of Athanasius by the sixteenth-century Anglican churchman Richard Hooker: "The whole world against Athanasius, and Athanasius against it." See *Of the Laws of Ecclesiastical Polity* 5.42.5, in *The Folger Library Edition of the Works of Richard Hooker*, ed. W. Speed Hill, vol. 2 (Belknap Press, 1977–1998).

Chapter 11 The Debate Rages On, Part 2

1. The comment is found in Gregory of Nyssa's *Oration on the Deity of the Son and the Holy Spirit*. I do not know of an English translation of this work, but the Greek is available in *Patrologia Graeca*, 46:557B. The translation quoted here is my own.

2. Philip Schaff, *The Creeds of Christendom: With a History and Critical Notes* (Harper & Brothers, 1877), 1:28–29. The text may be read online at https://ccel.org/ccel/schaff/creeds1.iv.iii.html.

3. Gregory of Nazianzus, *Oration 31.10*, in *NPNF2*, ed. Philip Schaff and Henry Wace (Hendrickson, 1894), 7:321.

4. When reading this word, we should not necessarily think of today's institution called the Roman Catholic Church. The term "catholic" comes from combining the Greek words *kath* and *holos*, meaning "according to the whole," that is, universal or worldwide. It was a long-standing Christian term with conceptual roots in the New Testament. The word *holos* is used to describe the Christian church in Acts 5:11; 15:22; Romans 16:23; and 1 Corinthians 14:23. When ancient people referred to the "catholic church," they meant to designate the church's worldwide unity, not a hierarchy in Rome with one leader at the top.

5. *Theodosian Code* 16.1.2, in *The Theodosian Code and Novels and the Sirmondian Constitutions: A Translation with Commentary, Glossary, and Bibliography*, trans. Clyde Pharr (Princeton University Press, 1952), 440.

6. Socrates Scholasticus, *Church History 5.6*, in *NPNF2*, ed. Philip Schaff and Henry Wace (Hendrikson, 1995), 2:120.

7. The house church was called the Church of Resurrection. It received its name after a pregnant woman fell out of its highest balcony and died; but after many prayers were said over her, she came back to life and her baby survived as well. The Church of Resurrection was famous for its dreams, visions, and miracles. Other people said its name meant that after the Arian heresy had taken root, Gregory "resurrected" the biblical view by teaching Nicene doctrine. Sozomen, *Church History 7.5*, in *NPNF2*, ed. Philip Schaff and Henry Wace (Hendrickson, 1995), 2:379.

8. *Theodosian Code* 16.5.6 quoted in R. P. C. Hanson, *The Search for the Christian Doctrine of God: The Arian Controversy, 318–381* (Baker Academic, 2005), 805.

Chapter 12 Triumph of the Nicene Creed

1. The churches which reject (or differ from) Chalcedonian Christology are the Assyrian Church of the East (the "Nestorians") and the Oriental Orthodox Churches (the "Monophysites," such as the Coptic

and Ethiopic churches). Both of these branches of Christianity accept the Nicene Creed.

2. J. N. D. Kelly, *Early Christian Creeds*, 3rd ed. (Bloomsbury, 2006), 296.

3. Theodoret, *Church History* 5.7, in *NPNF2*, ed. Philip Schaff and Henry Wace (Hendrickson, 1892), 3:135.

4. Theodoret, *Church History* 5.7, in *NPNF2* 3:135.

5. Kelly, *Creeds*, 304.

6. *Council of Constantinople, Canon 1*, in *NPNF2*, ed. Philip Schaff and Henry Wace (Hendrickson, 1900), 14:172.

7. "The Nicene Creed," *Book of Common Prayer Online*, www.bcp online.org/HE/he2.html. See chapter 13 for discussion of the added italicized phrase.

8. Sara Parvis, "Constantinople 360 and Constantinople 381: A Tale of Two Councils," *Studia Patristica* CII (Peeters, 2021), 171.

Chapter 13 Later History of the Nicene Creed

1. Ambrose, *Letter 21A.1*, in *NPNF2*, ed. Philip Schaff and Henry Wace (Hendrickson, 1900), 10:430. The sermon is called *Letter 21A* because it is normally inserted into a collection of Ambrose's letters about these events.

2. Ambrose, *Letter 21A.1*, in *NPNF2* 10:430.

3. Tertullian, *Against Praxeas* 4; Ambrose, *On the Holy Spirit* 1.11 .119–120.

4. Basil of Caesarea, *On the Holy Spirit* 18.45; Cyril of Alexandria, *Thesaurus* 34; Maximus the Confessor, *Responses to Thalassios* 63; John of Damascus, *Dialogue Against Manichaeus* 5.

5. Other important verses include John 7:39; 14:26; 20:22; Acts 2:33; Romans 5:5; 1 Corinthians 2:12; and Galatians 4:6.

6. Augustine, *On the Trinity* 15.27–31, 37, 47–49.

7. "The Ecumenical Creeds," Book of Concord Online, bookofcon cord.org/ecumenical-creeds/.

8. "Belgic Confession," Christian Reformed Church, https://www.crc na.org/welcome/beliefs/confessions/belgic-confession.

9. "The Holy Eucharist: Rite Two," Book of Common Prayer Online, https://bcponline.org/HE/he2.html.

Chapter 14 The Trinity as the Gospel

1. "Meanwhile the cross comes before the crown and tomorrow is a Monday morning." *The Weight of Glory* by CS Lewis © copyright 1949 CS Lewis Pte Ltd. Extract used with permission.

2. Michael Reeves, *Delighting in the Trinity: An Introduction to the Christian Faith* (IVP Academic, 2012), 31.

3. Michael Reeves, *Overflow: How the Joy of the Trinity Inspires Our Mission* (Moody, 2021), 29.

4. Karl Barth, *The Humanity of God* (Westminster John Knox, 1960), 47, 49, 50. I have adapted the text by lowercasing the divine pronouns, as is more often done today in modern publishing style.

BRYAN M. LITFIN is the author of *The Conqueror* and *Every Knee Shall Bow*, as well as several works of nonfiction, including *Wisdom from the Ancients, Early Christian Martyr Stories, After Acts*, and *Getting to Know the Church Fathers*. A former professor of theology at the Moody Bible Institute, Litfin earned his PhD in religious studies from the University of Virginia and his ThM in historical theology from Dallas Theological Seminary. Bryan is professor of theology in the Rawlings School of Divinity at Liberty University. He and his wife have two adult children and live in Lynchburg, Virginia.

Connect with Bryan:

BryanLitfin.com

🅕 Bryan.Litfin